Athlete

Using Your Instincts to Play the way Nature intended

Lessons from life show you how

By Frank Adams

Over the years, teaching fundamentals passed down from one pro to another - especially for tennis and golf - have had little to do with the fundamentals of a natural athlete, or of how an athlete performs. Compared to that athlete, methods taught are awkward, ungainly and unusual. So you end up playing that way thinking the natural athlete has special gifts you don't possess. Happily you're about to discover that isn't true.

About The Author

Frank Adams, the originator of Natural Tennis, is the former owner of the trademark for Natural Golf. Frank has demonstrated his Natural Tennis techniques on ABC, NBC, CBS, PBS and syndicated programs such as the American Trail. A native of Connecticut, he was the Tennis Director and Head Professional at the New Haven, Milford, and Old Saybrook Racquet Clubs and has served as Chairman of the Department of Community Affairs for the Connecticut Pilot Tennis program. The author of Teach to Teach, a guide for physical education instructors, he formally wrote a newspaper column on Natural Tennis for the Milford Citizen.

Copyright © 2013 by Frank Adams All rights reserved. No part of this publication may be reproduced, stored in a retrieval system, or transmitted, in any form or by any means, electronic, mechanical, photocopying, recording, or otherwise, without the prior written permission of Frank Adams. Photography by Bob Becker.

Dedication

This book is dedicated to the memory of my good friend (Tom Cole) who embraced the techniques of "The Unconscious Athlete" to overcome age and debilitating illness, and then to perform more brilliantly than when he was a kid. Tennis practice with him was priceless. His heartfelt comments during those sessions are added to the text for you to enjoy.

Acknowledgments

The suggestions and writing skills of George Feifer are reflected throughout the book. His input has provided immeasurable flavor to the text. Add to that the editing know-how and watchful eye of Edward Letteron, and Nancy Chute, and encouragement from Paul Manson, along with the promotional skills of Harry Moses and Dean Adams. Finally, the catalyst to bring this project to the finishing line was the professional communication and input from Bob Becker, technical skills of Bruce Taylor, and the financial support of Valerie Friedman. My heartfelt thanks go out to all of them.

Table Of Contents

About The Author ii
Prologue vii
The Principles 1
Relating To The Natural Athlete 3
Playing By Feel 7
Playing The Way Nature Intended 11
Reacting 19
Recalling And Using Your Instincts 21
    Excuses
    Bad Reactions
    Review (A Snapshot to Finding your Natural Abilities)
Seven Habits And Instincts 25
    1- The freedom to forget what you're holding
    2- Reading the ball and letting it tell you how to hit it 27
    Anticipation vs. Reaction
    3- Measuring your body to the ball 32
    Drop hits
    4- Drift and stride 36
    Avoiding the shuffles and split steps
    5- Let your body do the organizing 39
    6- Shot sense (The key to eliminating unforced errors) 43
    Shot selection
    Using shot selection for doubles and singles
    7- Rhythm, timing and balance 48
        Warm- ups
        Tying instincts together
        Concentration vs. Awareness
        Hitches and Glitches
        Mental and Physical Balance
        Disconnects

A Game In Confusion 55
Traditional versus Contemporary Tennis
The Natural Approach 61
    (7) Catches and Throws
    Trouble Shooting
    The wobbles
    Overdoing
Parting Shots 69
    Enjoying the Game
    Playing in the Zone
Addendum 73

Prologue

Most of the physical skills you learn in life become "ordinary and routine". Barely do you think about how to perform them. But that's not so when learning a sport. Tons of lessons and practice that promise great improvement rarely produce them. Playing skills only marginally improve because lessons rarely relate to anything familiar. In fact, sports techniques are riddled with unusual movements and with thoughts that tend to paralyze the body.

But, hope is eternal. If rackets aren't broken in frustration or clubs thrown over the brink for similar reasons, dogged athletes will continue to chase the impossible dream of performing more proficiently. A dream which can only be reached when sports are taught the same way you learn to move in life. Inherently by instinct! When instincts are coupled with movement one knows and owns, a once - complicated sport becomes a normal activity which enables you to move with the grace and ease of a natural athlete. That's when playing your favorite sport will become more unconscious-routine, and more like how you stroll or amble down the street.

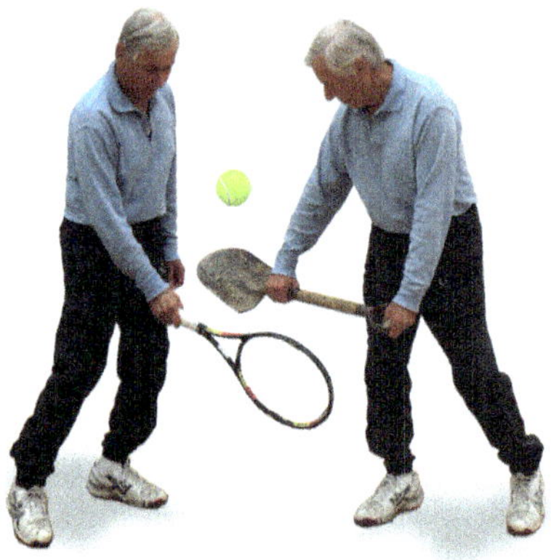

The Principles

This book's principles come from life. They illustrate the perfection you've attained to walk, dance or work. Perfection that will become synonymous with how you'll learn to play: Racket, bat or club... shovel, rake or broom...flute, drum or piano, you'll discover that the laws for perfecting one skill pertain to all. So are the rhythm, timing and balance utilized for each the same. The same required for golf swings and serves: two impostors that are alike, the difference being that one swings down and the other up. But both require the freedom, ease and timing of a musician.

Few know how to attain it. Tiger Woods, Annika Sorenstam, Jack Kramer and Roger Federer are exceptions. Kramer, who could knock cigars out of people's hands with his serve, certainly knew. So will you as you learn to play by feel and without thought, like those athletic giants...The way concert pianists play without needing to look at the key board... Or the way stenographers think in sentences, not words, to do the same. What about great athletes? They leave their minds in hotel rooms when going out to play. That's what this book's fundamentals are designed for you to do. They will remind you of long forgotten instincts, and provide the essential keys for you to play more like the athlete you admire. Primarily tennis oriented, these principles pertain to all sports and are easy to apply to yours. Enjoy!

Relating To The Natural Athlete

How would you like to float in the air with a basketball like Michael Jordan, swing a golf club with the ease of Annika Sorenstam, or play tennis with the brilliance of Roger Federer? Better yet, to "float like a butterfly and sting like a bee" like Mohammed Ali said he did in the ring. What's their secret?

The natural athlete doesn't walk, run up stairs, or tie his shoes any better than you. Some readers might even be faster and stronger. So why can't they play with the elegance, grace and simplicity of great athletes? It took me "only" 50 years as a tennis pro and coach to discover that by developing a natural athlete's mindset, you CAN. A mindset that eliminates the unusual and uncomfortable "techniques" we often use for playing a sport, then trading them for how we learned to ride a bike or catch a ball.

How did we learn those things? By rote, feel, total freedom, composure, mostly on our own, or by observing others. But how we were taught a sport was anything but easy, smooth, graceful, or simple. No, the fundamentals taught were different, difficult, and mostly unlike our daily routine. Outstanding athletes are able to overcome that cumbersome and difficult stuff. But they can't play without grunts and groans. Conversely, natural athletes aren't burdened by the moves of some "so called" expert. That's what makes them different. For example:

Natural athletes don't over think. We admire their ease, grace, and simplicity of play. Especially striking are their moves that seem to be no different than those we use on a daily basis. Unfamiliar grips, stances, and swings that take endless concentration to coordinate are seldom in their repertoire.

Conversely, the majority of athletes have to meditate on every move. They have excess baggage that will hang around like a deformed arm or leg, plaguing them for the rest of their days. A mind cluttered with disabling information is what prevents them from achieving their full potential.

In golf, it's called paralysis of analysis. With 15 things to think about, what else could it be? The excess baggage most teaching pros burden you with guarantees your moves will never be natural in any sport. So drop acquired notions of how to play. Then listen to your body and let it tell you how to move. You know, ordinary stuff done simply, with rhythm, timing and balance. More like how you walk and work, or the way a ball is snagged out of mid-air. Although there's nothing unusual about that, it's one of the most coordinated and athletic moves you can make. Your eyes pick up the flight and speed of the ball like radar. Then your hand instinctively shoots out to snag it in your finger tips. Truly a remarkable feat performed naturally, normally, with total freedom, composure, ease, and virtually "unconsciously".

As you can see, the right things happen when you move instinctively. But none of those good things will take place until you abandon distorted techniques that boggle the mind, destroy ordinary movement and the laws that flow from nature.

So drop the contorted and confusing stuff. Stuff like ordering yourself to use the right grip, turn sideways, bend your knees, keep your eyes on the ball, shift your weight, follow through, etc.

How to send those orders and react to them in the micro-second it takes to hit a ball? You can't! So rather than burdened with disabling information, you're about to learn how to relax and allow your wiser instincts determine your reactions.

Here's how: Forget that sometimes contradictory and always intimidating liturgy. Let play become routine and no different than it was before you picked up a sporting implement. And no different than the way you feel when your arms synchronize with each step you take. In other words, learn to "let your body teach you how to move". Then inject the routine and rhythmic movements of life into your sport. You'll be astonished by the good things that will happen.

But until now, you've had no chance to move so comfortably in a sport. One step onto a court, course, or playing field is all it took to forget how you walked before. Suddenly you're tense. A sports implement becomes alien and challenging. Familiar habits which enable arms and legs to work

Relating to the Natural Athlete

in synch with your body disappear. Futile compensation causes a rash of bad reactions.

You spend years trying to perfect movements and techniques that violate nature. Try all you want to make them normal, it's impossible! Movement, rather than fluid and graceful, becomes anything but elegant.

Why? That's because during the first five minutes of instruction, you depended on others to tell you how to move. Your instincts for normal movement were instantly lost. Strange grips, awkward and unfamiliar stances were accepted. Any athletic prowess you may have had turned into a disheveled mess.

Tons of practice will make you good only at doing things the hard way. But the day never comes without grumbling or berating yourself about some complex technique you've never gotten a handle on. How much fun is that?

So here's a question for you. Regardless of playing ability, the sport you play, or years invested in improving your game, what would it take to eliminate the frustration of disappointing performance?

Now's your chance! It boils down to how you want to feel when performing: choppy and by the numbers, or in a smooth, striding, drifting and floating way? Really, it's totally up to you.

To be natural, unconscious, and play in the zone, you must go back to the comfortable mental and physical things you hardly remember learning and even less about how you do them. Recalling them to memory will open your mind to how strange many of the ways you've been taught have always been. That's when you'll understand the following comment tennis impresario and legend Ilie Nastase made. When asked: "How do you play?" He responded: "I play the way I practice, like I don't care." Don't care? The wisdom in that statement doesn't mean not to care, but to disengage from becoming rigid, or trying too hard. So like Ilie, as in any sport, keep it simple by trading-in tension for composure and ease.

What about the years and tons of practice you may have done to improve play. Throw that away? Years of practice to improve are a mere drop in the bucket compared to the movements you've unconsciously performed zillions of times over the years.

So rather than learn unfamiliar techniques, drop those that, like a disease, cause frustration. Return to your old, very familiar ways. They far outweigh those you constantly have to think about. That will free you from a straight jacket of harmful advice. Who else would benefit from being free from such diatribe?

- Duffers with hope of being rescued from an epidemic of horrific swings and contorted positions.
- Enthusiasts who'll learn they know more about how to move in a sport than they thought.
- Seniors, rather than prematurely trade their rackets in for clubs, will jump for joy to perform with less effort... learn the ageless "walking game" ...or use tennis for therapy as the great Rod Laver, winner of two Grand Slams, may still be doing today.
- As for professionals: They'll play more proficiently.

With little more thought than breathing, when you learn to make life's comfortable moves sporting ones, play can be elevated to a level that's not only free but fun. It's not rocket science, but merely a matter of eliminating interference from your mind and trusting the gifts you already possess: Those which enable you to make "your only shot" the best one with the least amount of effort.

Playing By Feel

The unconscious athlete plays more by feel than by thought. Play for them is no different than a game of tag is for you. Unlike most athletes, they don't need an eternity to understand how normal it is to play. Innately they know. Without physical or mental hang-ups, so will you: Especially when the only thought on your mind will be to float and use your God given rhythm, timing, balance. Then without muscles rippling, anxiety or tension, you'll move smoothly as silk and be playing by "feel". You know, like the golf pro who lets "Mr. Callaway to do the work", or Michael Jordan on the court, Ali in the ring, Mario Le Mieux in the rink. So what's not to admire. For instance:

At five, Tiger Woods was too young to learn from books, or to fill his head with professional jargon. Neither mind nor body interfered with the swing he was born with. It's essentially the same swing Ted Williams used with a bat. The same Evonne Goolagong and Maria Bueno use with a racket. Who are the ladies just mentioned?

They're two of the most graceful and effortless performers of all time. Their liberated swings are identical to those gifted athletes use to wield bats or clubs, and no different than how workmen swing shovels, rakes or brooms. Once you see the parallels, never again will you allow a worried mind or tensed body interfere with the natural swings you own. The way legendary, Romanian superstar/super-brat, Ilie Nastase continues to do. Even now, well past his prime, out of shape, overweight, muscles and bones aching...Ilie's natural flair is therapeutic and continues to enable him to float ever so smoothly on the court. You know, the way you did before stepping onto it.

During the 1970's which seem like a lifetime ago, watching Ilie at Wimbledon, or just hitting balls with a lissome lady friend at a country club, his moves were harmonious and synchronized, and just as you should, the man continues to play by feel and has fun. "A genius with a racket" is the way John McEnroe categorizes him.

Yet, Ilie's movements mirror those you've naturally developed to perform a prosaic task such as to push open a door. That, like Mc Enroe's "so called" spaghetti grip (spontaneously learned) enables John to pickup half volleys and shoe string shots like a short stop. Because of it "no mans land", a plague for others, doesn't exist for John who can handle shots from anywhere. That enables him to move in, push opponents back, and take advantage of the court. Not needing to avoid certain parts of it offers tremendous advantage over the vast majority of opponents with styles that make them play "off" more than "on" the court. In other words, well behind the baseline. Their court, opened up like a parking lot, allows John to move in, push opponents back, and end boring rallies by angling balls away... Not with power, but deftly.

Hopefully, a day will come when a female version of McEnroe will enter the scene to tame powerhouses like the Williams sisters. They should be congratulated for the power of their game. But we've seen enough of it. As Roger Federer occasionally demonstrates, power is only one aspect of tennis.

Today, whoever has the best punch wins. How boring! Whatever happened to artistry and feel? To tame power, play must be versatile and free. Then it becomes fascinating and great stuff to watch. With a few minor adjustments in your thinking, you could play that way.

Whatever the sport: to play by feel means to get the greatest output from the smallest input. I call that the "feel good" way of honing your skills. Effortless skills you'll appreciate. Especially on days when you're not up to par, or as Joe DiMaggio said, "When your mind says do and your body says ouch"...Then what should you do? Play without angst! Above all, play according to how you feel. Some days that'll be with vim and vigor. Then on days when energy is waning, don't waste what you don't have. Conserve it by staying as cool, calm and collected as possible. The way my brother Happy always did to make him marvelous at golf and a high handicap bowler.

Lesson from life
(Composure)

Never having taken a lesson, Happy just gravitated to a sport. Totally composed, he didn't have an ounce of angst. Can YOU say that? When Happy, who's real name is Ray, picked up a tennis racket for the first time, he didn't know how to miss. Mumbling "This game is boring", he tossed the racket aside and walked away. Likewise, Moe Norman, a peculiar Canadian golfer, considered by some as the greatest all time striker of the ball, after demonstrating his skills blurted out, "This game is easy." Then dropped the club and did a Happy. You should be so lucky.

As lucky as a friend, a wonderful athlete, when in his seventies and battling illness, Tom Cole felt fortunate to be playing at all. The "traditional" game for him was no longer possible, nor desirable if he were able to play it. By relying on his God-given instincts, and using minimal effort, allowing his body to organize the racket, and like all great strikers of the ball, he even had time to pause before the racket dropped the weight of his body onto the ball. Tom's shots were more effective than when he was a kid. Even on days when most of his energy was sapped, he'd play the "walking game". Like chess, it's a game of placement and position which not only is satisfying, but can also be very effective.

Finally, to play by feel, you must adopt a mindset which enables you to move as comfortably with a racket, bat, or club as you do without them. You achieve that by injecting the way you move in life into your favorite sport. That's when you'll see how seamlessly life and sports fit together.

Happily when life's movements and instincts become sporting ones, no longer will you have to drag around the excess baggage others have hung onto you. Because now, athletic moves won't be cumbersome or unusual but the same as those you've always known. So let's look at how simple habits like walking and working become the same as playing ones.

Perfect Forehands and Backhands from the Beginning of Time

Playing The Way Nature Intended

Walking Habits

Unclenched hands allow arms to swing back and forth with each step you take. The arms also help wind and unwind your body. Only idiots would clench their fists and attempt to walk. Try it yourself. Where do your arms go? Nowhere! Stiff as a board, you'd have to pull them back as most players tend to do.

With grips on the brain, the tendency is to prematurely squeeze the handle of the sporting implement you're holding. You wouldn't do that to work, so why would you to play? No, you cradle working implements. Then without thought, the grip occurs the instant contact is made with the object you want to meet. There's nothing unusual about that. It's just a natural process. But beware! The slightest grip before making contact will stifle a free flowing performance. So don't let a little thing like that prevent your arms from moving as fluidly as they should. Otherwise, your days will be spent thinking and chiding yourself on how to get them back. "Racket back", remember?

Working Habits
Using Normal Habits and Instincts to Play

Tennis, baseball or golf, the scythe is the ideal tool to translate how working habits become playing ones. So pay close attention to the following illustrations. Then imitate them for easier and better use of a sporting implement.

The scythe is an ancient tool, once used on farms throughout the world. Its design conforms to the basic laws of physics and is ideal to demonstrate working habits.

Also almost impossible to misuse, working with it provides ultimate freedom of motion. Notice how the handles are precisely located. One is perfectly positioned to produce a forehand...the other, a backhand. With no demanding list of things to do, the workman lightly holds onto the handles of the scythe. Reads his work and comfortably steps onto the foot that measures him up to it.

The loosely held scythe automatically swings back as the body winds over and onto one foot. Then it freely swings the weight of the body off and onto the other foot. Get that! Without any help from you, it FREELY SWINGS THE WEIGHT OF THE BODY OFF AND ONTO THE OTHER FOOT! Then, without thought, it is automatically gripped the instant it cuts into the grass. Notice how both body and tool work together - precisely the way Annika Sorenstam and any other good golfer swing a club.

Everything else being equal, clubs differ from scythes, rackets and such, because the body, rather than walk or run over to a ball, addresses it by standing sideways. Lumberjacks do likewise to fell a tree. But unlike our golfing friends, their bodies are relaxed. That allows the ax to do the organizing. Golfers should take note and allow the club to do the same for them.

But even with practice swings galore, most golfers find that impossible. Because the second a ball is addressed, a subtle change of mind and body occurs, one a teaching pro may fail to catch. That's when the free flowing practice swing they may have had tightens and disappears. It's hard to believe, but overlook such a tiny detail and you'll never be able to take that practice swing out to the course. So when playing golf, set up like a lumberjack. Then with zero tension, let the club do its work.

However, placing two hands on a racket, bat or club is less comfortable than using a scythe. Rather than being ideally positioned, both hands touch. In no way is that as comfortable as when hands are apart. Prove that for yourself by putting them together. Notice the tension between your shoulders. To relieve it, some ball players release one hand from a bat after contact. That may be why Pete Sampras abandoned his two handed backhand.

Now let's take a look at how walking and working habits become playing ones.

Playing Habits

Just as the man with his scythe walks into position to work, you should do the same for sports. Remember, you're an expert at measuring up to things. You've been doing that all of your life. So why stop now? The same thing happens when you run to catch. You simply land onto the foot that comfortably measures you up to the ball. That's no different than with any object you want to meet or hit. When perfectly measured up to a ball, that's the instant to unclench your hands. Then drift and stride up and over to it like you do for anything else. And whatever you're holding onto will automatically be organized and gripped upon contact. But if you stop (or set-up) so will your arms, so keep moving! Then you'll move just as fluidly and freely as when off the court, course, or playing field.

Finally, forget all the mumbo-jumbo about setting-up. What a farce! There's no better way to slow you down, or destroy rhythm, timing and balance. What's best is to drift, stride and float over to the object that you want to meet. Normal movement is graceful and saves tons of time. Use it! Then like Andre Agassi, Ted Williams and great strikers of the ball, instead of being rushed, you'll be able to pause before making your shot. And at times, even feel that you could comb your hair before making your play. I call doing those things the "pause that refreshes." Relative to that:

Fred Perry, the great English player said that how the game is taught wasn't how he had played it. Grim contemplation, Herculean effort, along with grunts and groans, had nothing to do with the marvelous freedom and artistry he knew. Good workmen utilize those skills as well. To some degree, so do you when raking the lawn. The correlation between work and play is amazing. So is the relationship of one sport to another. The following story makes that point.

In the early eighties, Jimmy Ballard, the great golf guru, and I compared my "Natural Tennis" moves to those he taught in golf. We were on the same page: the moves of both sports were identical.

So much so that Jimmy talked about doing a video to illustrate the similarities with golf, tennis, and baseball.

But maybe you believe, as I once did, the "old wives tale" about playing one sport hurting the other. That's hogwash! Apply the basic laws of physics to any sport and the similarities will surprise you. Why should that be? Because at work or play, the law of gravity dictates that there's but one best way to perform. How great it would be if the sporting world used the laws that govern the universe as their guide!

Unfortunately, few know what rackets, bats and clubs are really for. As for shovels, rakes or brooms, nobody needs tell you how to use them because the work they're made to do is easily identified. Without needing to be told, your hands naturally fall into place for you to swing them.

Nevertheless, few strikers of the ball can identify their work which makes it impossible for them to know when, where, or how to utilize what's in their hand(s). That's especially true with a racket. No one seems to understand the right way to hold or swing one anymore. At least with a bat or club, it doesn't take rocket science to know two hands are needed to swing them. But just a few years back, the tennis profession thought they'd cornered the market on how to do it. Apparently, they missed the boat because today, the ugly and gut wrenching styles once laughed at win major titles, much the same as the traditional "foot shuffling" ones of the past.

Take Roger Federer for example, when without a coach, he neither used the traditional or contemporary techniques. "I move differently", he would proudly say. Differently meaning by instinct and the way advocated in this book.

Who could improve on such brilliant play? Mistakenly, Roger thought others could. Leaving his instincts behind, he allowed his game to be tinkered with by renowned coaches. Then players who had never beaten him did so. Thankfully Roger's discouraging performance was short lived. Once again, he has regained most of his former brilliance. To learn more about some of the convoluted stuff Roger may have gotten into, turn to "A Game in Confusion" (on page # 57).

The good news is that we all have inherent natural abilities. To release them is like a spiritual experience. Abilities that open your eyes, free you from rigid rules, and allow you to react instinctively to control play rather than for it to control you.

During my coaching years, I observed how both fledgling athletes and professionals get hung up on conventional rules. Those that don't match-up to the lifetime of familiar ones you know. Having forgotten them, the old you with tons of experience, will adopt methods that are new and strange. Little wonder they get bungled up and abilities go down the drain. But to get back on track, all you need to do is to be yourself, study the moves you know, and use them to perform. Then you'll leave the tortured moves that cripple mobility behind. Take my cousin Boo for example:

Lessons from life
(Dependence versus Self Reliance)

There was nothing wrong with the big strong boy, or the way he lumbered around. That was okay with us, but not with his mother who wanted him to walk with a normal gait like the rest of us kids. So she taught him how to walk with awful results.

Boo was a good man. The old gang remembers him fondly, even if he never learned to walk our way. Neither would you, if at the age of ten, totally capable but lacking confidence, you called your father to tie your shoes and comb your hair. Totally dependent upon others, don't we do the same in sports? The following story shows that we do.

The first time I picked up a golf club was after selling my trademark for Natural Golf. At first, casually hitting a ball around was easy. So was my first shot off the tee, long and down the middle. The "Wow" from the professional playing with me was all I needed to hear. Full of confidence and playing by instinct, I found a club no harder to use than a grass-whip or broom. That was until the next shot when my casual, cocky attitude got in the way. God only knows how bad it was. Nonetheless, it was the perfect invitation for my friend, the pro, to bestow his vast reservoir of knowledge upon me.

That's the instant I gave up my instincts. No longer would I be able to identify normal movement or correct a problem because: grips, stances, and swings would now be different than those I knew. That summer, the graceful moves I knew went down the drain. The trust I had in myself was gone. Play became engineered and tortured. Did I feel like Boo? You bet I did!

Now, like my cousin, I'd have to depend upon others to tell me how to move. Stooping to a new low, I accepted a batch of golf videos which promised help but compounded the problem. I threw them away. Exasperated, what should I do? Hack away for the rest of my life like most of my cronies? Or face the problem like a man?

Mustering courage, I went back to instincts. And with a few reminders, you can reestablish yours a whole lot sooner. The way a farmer showed me, ages ago, on how to use just about every tool in creation. He had no conscious idea about instincts and even less did I. Still, I learned to fell trees, to use crowbars, to swing scythes and pitchforks, to handle hay, to wield sledgehammers, to you name it. That took eight short weeks.

All I learned in tennis during the same amount of time was an adequate forehand. As with golf, I was given myriads of things to think about. It would take a minor miracle to play the game at all. Yet, my adequate forehand was enough to get me into the finals of a junior tournament. I was fifteen. Friends and spectators knew my opponent had never beaten me. But now he had me five games to love, triple match point, and I was playing like a nerd. That's why my Canadian coach liked to call me "Citron", French for lemon. Because he was used to seeing me play with a dash of brilliance one minute and like a buffoon the next. Smiling, he mumbled "Citron, what happened?" I didn't know. All I knew was that this was my Wimbledon.

Somehow, I managed to stave off the three match points. Stupidly, I thought the pressure was off. Losing the next point made it match point again. That brought me back to reality. Eyes like saucers glued to the ball, I pitted my backhand against his weaker one. But the devious competitor pulled out a fine drop shot. Slipping while returning it, down on the clay, gazing up as his callous return sailed over my doomed head, I knew it was over. My opponent prepared to run up and gallantly shake my hand. But just before that happened, something within me took over. Adrenaline flowing, I was up in a flash, tracked the ball and made a return that dribbled over the net. Nobody believed their eyes, certainly not my opponent who went on to lose the point - and then, still in shock, the match.

What's the moral of the story? I didn't make the shot that saved the day as much as it made itself. It happened instinctively, immediately, without an ounce of conventional thought. Here was a habit and instinct my farmer teacher inherently knew, along with others you're about to learn. Reminded of and using them to play, will guarantee that your knees won't be bloodied like mine when you receive your trophy. Nor will you be as ignorant about how you did it. That's when play will become close to how it is for you to breath, and the same as it is for you to walk. No longer different, playing a sport then becomes identical to the comfortable and graceful things you know and do in life. Then, like Morihei Ueshiba, that's when you'll simply react!

Reacting

Morihei was the grand master of the self defense exercise called Aikido. He excelled at turning the strength of opponents against them. Ushiba, in his eighties and barely five feet tall, found the speed, bulk, and strength of others no match for his efficient reactions. They were the same reactions that enable Zen archers to snag arrows in mid-flight...the same you use when crossing the street...the same needed to return 120 mph serves, and the same Arthur Ashe used to overcome the great James Scott Connors at Wimbledon in 1975. Almost trance-like that day, playing the best tennis of his life, Arthur got the most out of every shot by using placement and position with minimum effort.

It was Ashe who said: "Yesterday, we had tennis players who weren't athletes. Today, we have athletes who aren't tennis players." What did he mean? There are few exceptions to that today. However, the answer to Arthur partly lies in Fred Perry's comment to me about "running making up for a lot of mistakes."

Too much attention is now focused on athletes who look more like track stars than tennis players. Much better are those who limit running... allow their natural reactions to take over...get the greatest output from the smallest input... and by playing placement and position.

What's placement and position? It's like playing a game of chess. Simply stated, you place yourself in front of an opponent's best return. Then force him to make an unwieldy one. That technique, along with DVD demonstrations of others, will enable you to reach the best you can hope for, the best you can do. Your full potential! Therefore:

Let movement become elegant, simple, unconscious, and with a natural flair your body feels good about. Like the pitching rhythm that Sandy Koufax and Satchel Page once used. Otherwise, when movements from life are left behind, play becomes tedious, ungainly, and difficult. Tons of practice and a lifetime of thinking (even for professionals), are required for many of the odd things you're expected to do. Doomed, you'll never stop mumbling and grumbling over what you should or shouldn't have done. So no matter how long you've played a sport, or how good you are, reminders of life's normal ways will help you to improve.

Recalling And Using Your Instincts

Instincts are so habitual that we're unaware of them. In fact, we hardly notice how our arms swing back and forth as we walk. Yet it's an instinct you perform as well as the best athlete. Unfortunately, unlike that athlete, the usual movements used in life are traded-in for the unusual. So, you end up looking and feeling like a freak. However, don't be embarrassed, it's the norm. But if you're a professional who's gotten good at doing what's uncomfortable, congratulations!

Even if you're a "great athlete" who can do summersaults and energetically perform at a high level, to reach your full potential and play with the ease of a "natural" athlete, you must use what you know and do best. Then, no longer will you worry about affected, guided, steered or hampered swings like those that occasionally happen when serves are out and don't count. Without an ounce of thought, cogitation, tension, or energy, that's when you UNCONSCIOUSLY zing back the most remarkable shot of your life. Remember? They're shots played purely by instinct, and great returns made simply by reaction.

If you're a beginner who hasn't had that experience, speak to those who have and marvel at the result. Because when returning to their unusual ways of playing, they find those wonderful shots impossible to duplicate. Why? The reason is because too many muscles (including the brain), were engaged.

Your ability to duplicate great shots will be proportionate to the amount of preparation and calculations you replace with your instincts to relax and automatically react.

Excuses

However, excuses will shoot your instincts down. "Old Tiger" my nickname for Ed van Beverhoudt, a New England tennis legend I've known for ages, was a sterling example of never having an excuse. Even when I was certain a late night would do him in, the tough competitor mustered up even greater determination than usual to dispatch his opponents.

Not all pros have that liberating quality. As a former head pro of the West Side Tennis Club and I recalled our younger days, we got a laugh from the excuses we once saddled ourselves with. For him, the slightest breeze was too great a handicap to overcome. Anyone could beat him on such a day. But when conditions were right, he could go five sets with the likes of Roy Emerson. My quirks were just as diminishing. I often played doubles matches with Fred La Liberty, my coach.

One time, our opponents were two old fogies who were drubbing us because I was playing without instinct. "Hey Citron, we can't lose to these guys," Fred said. Oh no? I kept preparing the reason.
I hadn't gotten my full complement of sleep, ate less than a nutritious breakfast, and took an inadequate warm up. How to forget such things? My wake up call was a stinging drive from Fred that nailed me on the back of the head. Forgetting everything but the embarrassment, I finally started to play.

How many excuses do you have? Satchel Page had the answer to almost all of them in his description of how it was like to be married to women half his age. "It's all mind over matter" he said: "If she don't mind, it don't matter." Remember that wisdom and don't buy into your opponent's gripes. Above all, forget your excuses. Just play the game with your body and its instincts, not your mental baggage. That's a tall order, but it requires no more than the perfection you've mastered in life, time and again. Tight rope walkers need that perfection even more. One misstep for them and it's over.
Although one misstep won't finish you off in a match...Omit one instinct and a rash of bad reactions will occur causing you to fumble.

Bad Reactions

For example: In tennis, Bill Tilden is blamed for fostering some of them. But he'd be tossing in his grave to learn the extremes to which his approach has been taken. Like the one which keeps ringing in players' ears

Recalling and Using Your Instincts 23

admonishing them to "get the racket back". No, Big Bill can't be blamed for that. All he really said was: "Take your racket back on the way to the ball". That's one "big" difference! But, there's no need even for that because, the racket will AUTOMATICALLY go back as you drift and stride toward it. However, if your body stops moving, or you squeeze the handle of a racket on your way to the ball, so will your arms. Then you'll have to pull them back.

Another misnomer to upset the apple cart is encouraging you to stand on the balls of your feet. What a joke! It's supposed to emulate a runner's starting position to quickly get off the mark. But it's nothing of the sort. All the tiptoe-ball tackling stance does is tie you up and tire you out. Look at it:

The stance makes it obvious that mind, along with the body and racket, are already engaged. Therefore, not relaxed or ready to react. Like a toad, you have to hop your body into action. What happens when you hop at the wrong time, or in the wrong direction?

But getting off the mark isn't complicated, or unusual. It's just the way you start out to walk. Simply leaning forward automatically engages your feet. With the blink of an eye you find yourself heading in the right direction to snag a ball, or to hit one away. Really, it's just that simple. Then, with great pleasure, no longer will you need to rack your brains remembering to:

- Bring your racket back
- Turn sideways
- Bend your knees
- Shift your weight
- Watch the ball
- Make contact
- Follow through, etc…etc…

Trying to remember those traditional canons and putting them in sequence makes playing a nightmare. But it's no different in any sport. No, that kind of mental and physical baggage is the problem and a sure-fire way to prevent playing in a normal and natural fashion. So how do you untangle yourself from all of that folderol? Your body is waiting. It knows how. It's only the mind that takes time to adjust. That's especially true if you've gotten good at doing things the hard way. Like religion, that stuff's not easy to give up.

Nonetheless, tons of practice pale into insignificance when compared to the comfortable and unthinking movement that you know. So what are you giving up? Movements riddled with embellishment, constraint and confusion. Instead, make the way you play reactive and automatic. Because, when a sport matches life, the confusing and awkward stuff stands out like a sore thumb. Stuff you'll drop like a hot potato once you make life's ways sporting ones. What follows should give you a head-start for finding them.

Review

Finding your natural ability boils down to relating to the effortless, nearly thoughtless things we do in life with hardly giving thought to having done them. Once identified, the next step is to inject them into athletic life. For example:

* Listen to your body. Let it be your coach. The normal moves it makes will reveal that you already know how to move efficiently, effectively and effortlessly.
* Utilize those normal movements when you play.
* Move simply and freely without a hitch. Then be mentally and physically composed with zero tension...Totally settled and at ease.
* Finally, adopt a mindset which enables you to move as comfortably with a racket, bat or club as you do without them.

What I've just described is night and day from the fundamentals used by 99% of athletes. Tension, over thinking, and insecurity are the norms. But detach yourself from those things. Learn to identify the instincts you own. Incorporate them into the sport you love. Then play will become equally as normal and routine as what you do in life.

Seven Habits And Instincts

Instinct # 1
(The freedom to forget what you're holding)

Ask Federer the last time he's thought about using a racket. Brand, string type and tension will be all that he'll remember because it's become part of him. That enables him to walk, run, catch and throw with a racket like you do without one. So stop the robotics...the contemplating of grips, or of swings and such things. Forget and allow the sporting implement you're holding to become part of you...Just like an arm or leg which has become oblivious. Let it become a perfect extension of your arms. Then, regardless of the sport, free your mind by paying less, rather than more attention to what's in your hand or on your feet.

Most importantly, learn to disengage from trying too hard. Why fight against yourself when all that's required to perform brilliantly is to:

- Take the path of least resistance
- Move in your normal and routine way
- Learn to pay less rather than more to what you are doing

That's what great strikers of the ball do. "You can hear the silence in their shots," as sports commentator Mary Carillo would say. Hopefully, someone will say that about you. Then you'll know you're in the zone. What zone?

A zone which allows you in a cool, calm and collected way, to produce the kind of performance you've dreamed of. One you can't duplicate when trying because too many sinews and neurons are activated. Instead, become like athletes who don't prod themselves with thoughts that bollix up performance. When going out to play, they leave their minds in hotel rooms. So will you when learning to pay no more attention to a racket, bat or club, than you'd expend on a shovel, rake or broom.

That's what gets you into a wonderful "be anxious for nothing" mode: One where you're virtually disengaged and no longer addicted to rudiments which break your game into pieces. For example: Thinking about grips, footwork, (you name it), is the same as dancing by the numbers and not to the music. It destroys your rhythm and freedom to float.

But to say it again, putting your hand on a sporting implement should be as instinctive as placing it on a garden tool. That's the first step for your game to come together in a spontaneous, free flowing and fluid way. You need to forget to the point of PAYING NO MORE MIND to what you're holding, or doing, than when walking. How much conscious effort on your part does that take? Yet walking doesn't prevent your arms and legs from synchronizing: Neither when playing a game of tag, snagging a ball, or flinging one away. Those things don't take a lifetime to learn or think about. But your arms and legs still operate. Just the way they should when playing. The paradox is that "no thought" will end up being your "best thought".

Unfortunately, only a handful of athletes naturally gravitate to the most comfortable way to hold and use a sporting tool. The rest have to fidget with stances and eternally meditate on their every move. Also, as you'll see, different grips will produce different swings. The more you twist them from a neutral - natural state, the more complicated and uncomfortable they become. Practice them "til the cows come home" but it won't help. Rather than grooved, each swing will have been planned, guided and steered.

Fortunately, you unknowingly have a natural swing. The job is to restore the swings you know to memory. Then use them without a tinge of "mental interference", an ounce of "cogitation", until moving in a sport becomes an extension of you, and more like arms or legs you forgot eons ago.

Finally, the less self conscious you are, the better. Maybe you remember a verbal or athletic response that surprised you because it was more inspiring than one you'd planned. Athletes and orators are no strangers to that experience. Bound by fundamentals (or notes) can virtually paralyze performance. Mind boggling are the times your best performance pops up when you mentally and physically forget yourself. Pat Cash did this to defeat Ivan Lendl at Wimbledon.

Flabbergasted as most of us were, all Ivan could say about the way Cash played was, "He just reacted." That's a necessary requirement for rapid response; one on that day which was a blessing for Cash. Otherwise, there was no other way he could have beaten such a formidable opponent, a player who has never been given due credit for his greatness. So like Cash, what should you do?

Rather than play carefully, play carefree because…A carefree attitude is much better than a careful one. Likewise, a playful attitude is more effective than grunts and groans that'll drag you down. Also, the harder you try the less you accomplish. For instance, like when paying too much attention to style rather than to the elegance of a simple, uncomplicated stroke. Finally, the right thing to do is… Disengage, be graceful, and glide around. Then, the drudgery of play will become magical.

Instinct # 2
Reading the Ball
(Let the ball tell you when and how to react)

Reading the ball reveals the traditional cart before the horse technique that, incredibly enough, allows a tiny ball to push you around. This occurs in tennis, baseball, or any sport when a player confuses anticipation with reaction. Thinking that anticipation is the same as reacting, the player reacts before reading the ball's spin, speed, and direction. That's like reacting before reading the red, yellow, and green of a directional light: A dangerous thing to do. Although reacting before you read a ball isn't as dangerous, you could end up being played by it. Not a pretty sight! The same happens to golfers and ball players who allow their minds to interfere with their swings. So what's right? "Read the ball"…Let it tell you when and how to react! This instinct (born of reaction rather than thought) is what will enable you to make beautiful shots. What shots?

The shots that happen with lightning speed and are much too fast to think about. Like when you drive a ball long and straight off the tee, over the wall from the plate, or sink a thirty foot basket. Unhampered by worry, you found your God-given rhythm, balance and timing. The same you use to dig with a shovel, clean with a rake, or sweep with a broom. Unfortunately by trying, you stifle your ability to duplicate such wonderful shots because you quickly revert to rigid stances, mental sweating, crippling grips, grim contemplation and calculating. But you're not alone.

Tennis pros have the same problem, but less in making great returns than in consistently duplicating a great performance. Thankfully, you can take the mystery from making wonderful shots along with others you only dream about by "reading the ball", and letting IT tell you when to react. That's what "Nasty" Nastase did to meet a ball with the butt of his racket and to confuse opponents by looking in one direction and hitting in another.

How to prepare for such shots? Not by grim concentration, but with total composure, physical / mental relaxation, and with an empty mind that can perform the unimaginable. Clogged minds and rigid bodies prevent swift reactions. So like Ilie, don't calculate how you're going to play a ball: At least, not until you read what your opponent or the ball is doing. Otherwise, to plan ahead for a shot that may not happen is a bad impulse that evokes compromised, pretzel-like swings. Then, just because of confusing anticipation with reaction, the ball ends up playing you. It's an athlete's worst enemy.

Here's the Lesson

Military recruits learn that lesson the hard way. How? When drill sergeants warn them to "listen up" and not to anticipate the command. One time is all it takes for an errant soldier to get the message by anticipating the command and doing an about face on "to the rear" before the actual command to "march" is given. You can only imagine the shock of looking directly into the eyes of 72 men who, a second before, were behind you. Don't ask me how I know. It's embarrassing! But it's the quickest way to clean out your ears. Next time from fear or shame, you instantly become attuned to "listen up".

Reacting to a ball before reading it is no different. Also, it's an instructional hazard that causes affectation and constraint – two enemies you don't need. Here's the scoop:

Unlike conventional tennis wisdom which confuses anticipation with reaction, anticipation merely means to expect - not react. Expect a traffic light to change, or expect a ball to be hit. What's different? Either way, your eye is expectantly on the light, just as it should be on the ball. As with any moving object, you field a ball by reading its speed, spin and direction. If it's a stationary one like golf, you react to a beautiful lay-up, or any other shot that you picture in your mind. Soo...Either way, total composure is required. But to intercept a moving object, such as a tennis ball... the micro-second before an opponent's return, you should already be ambling forward to intercept it. Doing that will empty your mind the way Zen archers do to snag arrows out of mid air. Because...

The mind reacts with the speed of light. The trick is not to let a bunch of neurons bollix it up. Often, the only time you have is to react, let alone think! One millisecond of thought that you may not have time for is diversion enough to muff things up in any sport. Yet, tennis players kid themselves into thinking they can plan 2 or 3 shots ahead. But for that to become possible, you have to be in control.

Players also delude themselves into thinking they have time to shape a shot on a screaming serve or stinging drive from an opponent. But the biblical expression "Enough to worry about today" aptly applies to any sport. Often a steaming shot, punch, catch, slap, or jump shot is all you have time for. To handle lightning returns, John McEnroe says it this way: "Stick out your racket and good things happen." What could be quicker? My friend Tom told me... "The best way to handle any shot is to become Buddhist like and take what God gives you." Great advice!

Strokes, pitches, drives, etc. should be fluid, free, naturally grooved, reactive, and not grimly contemplated to tie your mind up with technique for eternity. Remember, a stroke should require no more thought than when using a scythe, or to make a simple catch.

Above all, before reacting, you should be free from mental and physical tension. Also, you should feel light as a feather and totally composed the way Zen archers free themselves by being calm and "letting go". The slightest angst or second guessing for them would risk catching an arrow between the eyes. No, regardless of what's thrown at you, do what great performers do. Become cobra-like waiting to strike and allow circumstance to tell you when and how to react. So, don't let your mind trip you up. Otherwise, when what you anticipate isn't what you expect, one punch is all it'll take to knock you off your feet.

Lesson
(Anticipation)

Eons ago, I watched a cocky Golden Glover bob, weave, and spar, only to waste meaningless punches: Punches which slid by the face of (former heavy weight) Jersey Joe Wolcott's old and toothless sparring partner. Patiently he watched each bob and weave, and with brilliant timing... one punch was all the old pro had to throw to end the bout. That happened in Marine boot camp to a drill instructor, hugely disliked, who took liberty and delight in knocking us around the ring. Still smiling, I'll never forget the glorious moment the egotistical punk was lifted off his feet and laid flat-out on his back. So take a tip from a pro, wait for your opening. Then with lightning speed, react when the opportunity presents itself.

Above all... Don't confuse anticipation with reaction, or you'll end up zigging when you should have zagged. But keep in mind that anticipation merely means to expect, the way a New York cabby does, poised and waiting for a light to change. The same goes for you. Anticipate, but don't guess! Again, for tennis, Johnny Mac's technique is to: Simply find the ball with his racket. A great technique! What about you?

Reacting

For right handed players a ball an inch to the right of your navel should be taken with a forehand. When one is an inch left, take it with a backhand. Lefties merely need to reverse the process.

What about shots hit directly at your mid section? Unfortunately, they're a nightmare for the majority of players. They're rare, but can be easy to handle either way. Unlike "Big Mac" who places the racket directly on the ball...rackets are pulled up and away from it. Now out of position, the ball becomes uncomfortable to play. But when used as an extension of your arm and hand, no ball is ever too close. So, here's how to play it:

Catch and throw the ball away with a racket, just like you'd do with your hand. Then shots at your feet become easy. Your newly found ability will allow you to move into the court, take balls on the rise, make winning angles, and easily put them away. In time, you'll learn to love those dreaded shots, even thankful when opponents hit them... Especially when balls are hit at your shoe strings. Without needing to take a step, it'll be a cinch to snag them with half volleys from anywhere on the court... including in no mans land!

That's an 18' area between base and service lines - at all costs tennis players are cautioned to avoid. Why? When you have the ability to handle any shot, it can be a wonderful place to be. Closer to net, you'll have more court to hit into. As for the opposition, they'll have less time to react. OK, what about watching the ball? That's a misnomer.

Now, knowing when to react, you can eliminate the shopworn mantra of watch the ball from your vocabulary. Without chanted reminders to yourself or any other conscious effort on your part, your eyes will be glued to it. Like when thrown a set of keys, you don't need your own voice or others to remind you to watch them. Because what tennis players, even golfers don't realize is: It's not the eye that's off the ball... it's the mind. So, don't strain eyes to watch the ball meet the strings of the racket. That's another old wives tale. For instance:

Catchers don't watch a ball slap into a glove... batters into the bat, nor did Rod Laver watch it into the strings of his racket. What really happens is... Your eyes pick it up like radar. Then, like a guided missile, your limbs are told where to intercept it. But Charlie's father, a good tennis player himself, took watching the ball meet the strings to the extreme. So he wove a rope into a circle, slightly bigger than a ball, onto the face of a racket. Supposedly to help his young son watch it make contact. Unfortunately, all it did was make the young lad cross-eyed. What the father should have told his son was: "Let the ball tell him when and how to play it". Then, Charlie's eyes would have picked it up the same as yours do to make a catch.

Finally, learn to read body language. Boxers and martial arts advocates pick it up in the eyes. Outfielders and tennis players read body language before a ball is struck. It's a tip-off that allows you to block a punch, or cut off a drive. Your body language can also be used to foil the opposition. In basketball, it's done by faking a move different from the one you intend. In tennis, you leave your alley open, lure the opponent to hit into it, and then close it off for a winner.

Instinct # 3
Measure your body to the ball
(The essence of balance)

Natural athletes get the most from the ball with the least effort. Nobody did that better than Ed Moylan, a 1950's tennis player who could hit a thousand, free flowing shots without missing. Try it sometime. It only takes an hour and fifteen minutes. It's a wonderful aerobic exercise if you can do it. Aside from being master at "measuring his body to the ball", Moylan utilized the instinct of "shot sense" to the 'nth degree. Like a concert pianist, no one opened up the court or played every inch of it more beautifully.

Ed was considered to have the greatest ground game of all time. Unfortunately, only those of us privileged to have seen him play know Ed. Hitting hard to him was like signing your death warrant. The harder you hit, the less he had to do to use your strength against you.

Proof of that was when he easily defeated Wimbledon Champion Dick Savitt, a strong serve and volley expert, on a wooden floor at New York City's 7th Regiment Armory. None of us thought Ed had a chance. After all, he wasn't a power player. His was a game of perfect timing and finesse. So the more you did, the less he had to do. Often, without time for the slightest back-swing or energy, Moylan simply put his racket on the ball to use Savitt's power against him. The result? Balls zinged past his marvelous net rushing opponent before he knew it. That was a fabulous feat on wood… the fastest of all surfaces. The ball screams off it. So fast that I once saw a serve bounce and hit a player in the Adams apple.

Thankfully, my first introduction to wood was a little more forgiving. All that happened to me was to get caught in the middle of my back swing. But hearing the ball thud into the wall behind me was a little disconcerting. Why? Because… unlike Moylan, I used a "traditional" backswing. So to better play on wood, my partner and I shortened them. But the major thing we tried was something called a "ballistic swing". A swing the author of the book by that title attributed to Laver. No way Jose! That twisted swing is more attuned to today's game of grunts and groans that have little to do with Laver or Moylan.

So how did those guys do it? They, unlike my cousin Boo, walked and ran up to the ball just like you would without anything in your hand. How did Boo do it?

Lessons from Life

Using the new glove his mom had just purchased, desperately hoping that it might insure a place for her boy on our sandlot team, my aunt asked me to play catch with him. Gladly accepting her request, I flung a hard-ball at him. Unfortunately, Boo placed the glove in front of his face. No longer able to see the ball, he removed it. Instead of finding the ball, it found him. But don't think talking about my cousin's ill fated moment is mean spirited. Although doubtful that it might have curtailed a baseball career, Boo enjoyed our cajoling him. But had he removed his face rather than the glove from the ball, who knows? As for you: When a ball comes directly at you which often occurs up at net - simply "fade" out of the way. The way Boo should have done to make a catch.

Like my ill fated cousin, trying to organize the racket, or yourself, before your body is in the right place is a "big" mistake. That would be like trying to shift gears before disengaging a clutch. You, like a car, need to be in neutral before you shift. Otherwise, your body, like a car's transmission, grinds against itself. But before you can get into neutral, you need to measure yourself up to a ball. How? The same way you measure yourself up to any object. Not by concentrating on footwork, but by walking or running onto the step which measures you up to it. In tennis, a good way to instill that instinct is to drop-hit. There's no better way to measure your body to the ball.

Drop Hits

Without much thought, players will drop a ball onto the court, either to send it for an opponent to hold, or to start a rally. But on the return, the ease with which they hit to begin the rally disappears. Take my friend Irving for example. As for his forehand, forget about it! God only knew the amount of thinking that went into it. However, when Irv dropped and hit a ball to me, his forehand was perfect. "Why don't you hit all of your forehands that way?" I asked. But it was a waste of breath. Thankfully, nobody taught Irv how to drop-hit. If they had, it wouldn't have been his best shot. But it's one you need to exemplify in order to hit yours. So here goes...

For forehands... face the net. Then point the foot closest to the ball into the direction you want to go... walk onto it... allow the racket arm to go into neutral... lift and drop the ball precisely as shown. Then, drift over to it. As you do, the racket will automatically follow and help to wind the body. When totally wound, the racket acts like a trigger. One that slowly or quickly, you control to unwind and propel the weight of your body into the ball. When properly timed, your step, hit and grip will happen simultaneously. But none of those good things will take place unless you stay "totally" relaxed and have precisely dropped the ball.

For backhands... face the net. Point and step onto the foot closest to the ball. Racket relaxed and in neutral. Then palm open, lift the arm straight up from where it hangs along your side. Next, allow the ball to roll off your finger-tips so that it will land sufficiently ahead of you. Otherwise, it'll be too close and you'll scrunch. When dropped in the right spot, simply drift over to it. Automatically, the racket will follow and help wind the body. Then trigger like, the speed of your swing will determine the amount of force and weight of your body that you want to pummel into the ball.

Drop-hitting to start a rally is great practice. It reminds you of how to measure yourself to a ball when playing. Like a mathematical equation, everything comes together, and even with eyes closed, you'd hit the ball. Look, if blind golfers can do it, so can you! Drop the ball too far forward though, and if you haven't interfered with the natural path and flow of your swing, it will go into the net. Not because you didn't bend your knees... but because you reached! Conversely, drop it too close, you'll scrunch, be cramped, and more likely than not, the ball will sail out of bounds.

For good things to happen, always start out facing the net. Not sideways to it as some may advocate. Stuck in position, that'll prevent you from moving in your usual way. As for arms, you'd have to "pull them back". Then cajole yourself into shuffling around, bending your knees and shifting your weight. A much easier way would have been to walk over to the ball and allow the racket to follow, as you float and measure up and over to it, just the way Roger Federer does so beautifully. But the first thing on your mind must be to "get" to the ball before thinking about hitting it. Just as you'd bring a broom up to what you wanted to sweep before starting to sweep. So "get" before thinking about "hitting"! But what about bad bounces, spins and balls affected by wind. How do you measure up to them?

By tracking them down the way Don Budge did, at age 53, during a ten game exhibition match with my good friend Edward van Beverhoudt on a New Haven, CT. football field. Along with spin and wind, you can only imagine the bounces they got. Nonetheless, with composure equal to that of Roger Federer's, Budge, regardless of where the wind blew, or how badly the ball bounced, never got set. But by drifting and striding, he tracked it down until his body was in position to hit. That was a marvelous demonstration. One equal to anything I've ever seen. Little wonder he was a grand slam champion.

Instinct # 4
Drift And Stride *Lessons from Life:*

My first job was as a 16-year old laborer in Sprague, Connecticut, the town where I grew up. Pete, a veteran farmer who served as the foreman, handed me a shovel. My first assignment was to load a pile of gravel into a brand spanking new "International" pickup truck. Proud as a peacock, Marco, the driver, backed up his "racing green beauty" for my baptism. "Load 'er up," he ripped: Then he settled down behind the steering wheel to enjoy a thermos of hot coffee and the morning paper. Life couldn't be better for him until, I let my first shovel fly.

Some of the rock and sand found its target, the truck bed. The remainder splattered like shrapnel off the cab, into the cab, and even onto Marco himself. To hell with the coffee, this was war! I survived thanks to Pete's intervention along with a reminder of an instinct I'd forgotten...One of drifting and striding. Having absorbed the lesson, my shotgun approach disappeared almost immediately because now, my arms worked with, instead of against me and... I could send a shovel full of anything precisely where I wanted. That's how you'll send a ball when you drift-stride, and allow your arms to work with your body to swing you away.

Striding, aside from a beating heart, is the closest thing to perpetual motion. We're rarely aware that our arms wind and unwind the body like a spring with each step we take. But as a reminder, striding stops and mobility is stifled when you set-up for a shot. For example:

You don't set-up to catch or to walk. No, you drift and stride. Arms and body work together and give you the freedom to float. So why give that habit up when you play? Nasty showed how tennis players get stuck in position when they set-up and pull rackets away from their body.

During the 1994 Volvo Championships in Connecticut, the Legends of Tennis were billeted at the New Haven Lawn Club aside from Wimbledon, is, probably the only club which still required whites on court. Veteran players, mostly from other clubs, dug their whites out of back drawers and paid 50 bucks to charity for the chance to hit with genuine great(s). Hopping from one court to another, they hit volleys with Laver, serves with Emerson, and ground strokes with Nastase.

Ilie started the happy players at the baseline where their years of traditional training were obvious. Diligently pulling their rackets back, they found things pretty comfortable there. Then, Ilie purposely hit short. Stuck with their rackets in the fence, and unable to move forward, his students either shuffled sideways or froze in place. Playful as usual, Ilie asked what they'd had for breakfast. It wasn't the cereal or fried eggs, but the mental and physical mechanics that they needed to digest. That's what stifled their movement. The cure would have been to move first, measure their bodies to the ball, and allow their arms to go into neutral. Then, by drifting and striding, the body would have organized the arms the same as when one skates or dodges pedestrians on the street.

However, no matter how far away from a ball you are, resist the temptation to reach for it with the racket. In fact, NEVER REACH with it! Instead, reach with your body by drifting and striding. Even at times, to the point of falling on your face. That kills two birds with one stone. 1- Not only would your body have organized the racket on the way to the ball. 2- It will propel your weight into it.

Some years ago, Nastase exemplified that technique in a match with Dick Stockton who was a much younger and fitter opponent. Grumbling "Everything hurts" loud enough for spectators to smile, Ilie moved his aching body in a way that was therapeutic and off-putting. For example, when driving a ball deep to Ilie's backhand, Stockton closed in for the kill. But Dick didn't see the gleam in the master's eye as he drifted the way a ski jumper gracefully leans over skis. Rather than reach, he allowed his body to organize the racket on the way to the ball. Without shuffling, that enabled him to make an effortless cross court pass.

Avoiding Shuffles And Split Steps

The shuffles - learn to hate them! Like radio static, they prevent smooth and graceful play. It happens when the body jiggles around to chase after a racket. The same thing happens when you see a golfer waddle around the tee.

Busy feet, listen to them and you'll learn to shun those shuffling feet. Leave them for dancing to the beat of 42nd. Street. I know, you've been told, and told again, to keep those poor feet moving. When you do, it's impossible to establish a solid foundation for the body to glide over. A jittery one takes its place. But, when hands are relaxed and your instinct is to "let the body organize the racket", and to drift and stride, it will automatically be prepared to greet the ball.

A quiet foot that you walk, stride, drift over and onto is what you want. It's the easy-natural leg work that is familiar and stabilizing. Also, it's the Holy Grail which prompts the flexibility to loosen you up. So regardless of the sport, rather than unstable feet, let them be your foundation. Especially be sure to forget split steps. I know that's sacred ground for the teaching profession. Better for you not to know what they are. Instead, lean – drift, or fade onto the foot that most directly and comfortably allows you to float over to your objective. The ground you cover and the quality of shots will astound you. The way former players Tony Roche, Stefan Edberg, and Owen Davidson astounded opponents with magical volleys.

(Drifting and striding for volleys)

Above all, whatever turf you're playing on, don't slide. I know on clay, there are players who swear by it. But rather than moving differently on various surfaces, drift, stride, and glide on all of them. Not only is that easier on you, it gives your body a chance to use the tool you're holding with less effort. Then, it's merely a matter of swinging off and into the direction the body has prepared for you to go. Best of all is that you won't need to slide on clay which, if you get to doing, can cause trouble. Why? Because it opens you up to injury when trying to slide on a hard court.

Bottom Line: This instinct will enable you to float into any kind of shot, along with a marvelous feeling that'll immunize you from being played by a ball. In 1991, Stefan Edberg (using this instinct) played the best tennis of his life to achieve a phenomenal win over Jim Courier in the US Open.

Three warm-up shots were enough to reveal that Edberg was in a special groove that day. Pete Sampras, considered the best player of his generation, has had several such stellar performances. But even the great(s) like Margaret Court, Martina, Steffi, Billy Jean, Althea Gibson, the William sisters, or too many other guys and gals to mention, aren't always able to sustain their natural and liberated ways. Nobody is perfect, or always "in the zone". Some unwanted event, mental or physical, usually gets in the way. Like a headache, it trips you up to do something stupid. But when you allow your body to organize your swing, it's like taking an aspirin which cures the problem.

Instinct # 5
Let Your Body Do The Organizing

It's your body that does the organizing, not your feet. Surprised? No need to be. The foot merely acts like the rudder of a ship to point you in a certain direction. Then, as in life, the body takes over just the way it does for you to walk, use a shovel, or step into the batters box to swing a bat.

But there are times when just the opposite is true. Like when you serve, drive a golf ball, or split a log. Then your arms play the major role in organizing you. The reason is that you have to stand sideways to do those things. But for now, let's deal with the multiple ways the body does the organizing. Say like when you step around a corner. Do you wrench your shoulders around to turn as many teachers advocate that you do in a sport? Absolutely not! Because as a ship flows in the direction of a tiny rudder, or like a diver's body follows the head, it's only natural for you to follow the direction your foot points you into. Then, as you stride, not only will you turn, more often than not, that little step will organize you to...

☛ Hit cross court: One simple lifelike step right, or left, is all it takes to head you into one direction or the other. With tennis, it'll organize you to hit cross court.

☛ Hitting down the line: The deeper you step, the more you turn. Hitting down the line is open to you when your body sufficiently turns. Also, to befuddle an opponent, it gives you the option to swing your body cross court.

Seven Habits and Instincts

☞ Run away backhands: What about run away backhands? Those Pete Sampras hits with his back to the ball and net. Even then, Pete demonstrates that hitting off the back foot (the one farthest from the ball) is natural because, it's the easiest way for the body to organize the arms, and a perfect demonstration of how the body prepares what's in his hand. It's a great shot that allows Pete to make brilliant returns when running down a high bouncing backhand. Who taught it to him? Speaking of himself, McEnroe said that nobody ever taught it to him. But now, I bet Mac uses it. Thankfully, you don't need Pete's mastery to hit a similar shot. Your body will naturally prepare itself for you to do so.

☞ Hitting off the back foot: That's a misnomer. However, Whitney Reed made a practice of hitting off the back foot which the teaching profession once condemned as verboten. But at times, it's the best way to let your body prepare your arms to hit certain shots. It was good enough for Whitney to be "top banana" in the United States in '64. So take it seriously!

☛ Sway or fade out of the way: Sometimes it's easier to drift onto the foot farthest from the ball by swaying or fading out of the way The result is an automatic "cross-over step" that puts more space between you and the ball to comfortably handle it. Because instead of having to run around a backhand to hit a forehand away from the opposition, fading is a much easier way to leave an opponent flat-footed. The other advantage of fad ing is that it also allows you to do the same with a backhand. It's a wonder this technique, used from boxing to baseball, has never been taught in tennis. Even golfers employ similar stances to hit out of difficult lies.

Hockey and badminton players excel at that sort of stuff. Yes, run away, drift, fade, cross over, or sway out of the way…All are bona-fide ways to let your body arrange and keep your arms in synch with it.

Try the moves that have been illustrated. You'll find them normal, expedient, and the best way to organize what's in your hand. The reason: Your body does the organizing. So don't let it disorganize you. Then all that's left for you to do is to allow the swing of the sports implement you're holding send the weight of your body into the ball. That will enable you to execute the most expedient and effective shot. Use those techniques and no longer will balls that cramp your style push you around.

Lesson from Life

Ed Moylan was the great, perhaps unconscious, expert at letting his body organize the racket. In the mid fifties, he demonstrated that wonderful gift in an exhibition match with Little Mo Connelly who had been the world's top woman player. Just a few years before, a freak accident on horseback prevented her from breaking every record. Although she stopped competing, Mo could still whack the ball, which, in this case, got lots of extra pace from the 25 mph gale blowing into Moylan's face. Undaunted, he still got the most out of every ball with the least amount of effort. That day, hitting his only shot, the most comfortable one, became more important than ever. Proving that less is more, he hit as deeply then as on the calmest day. Like a workman wielding a shovel, Ed allowed the racket to throw the weight of his body into each ball. Just the way you would to throw out a bucket of water.

The key to this instinct is to enable the body to organize your arms the way you did as a kid. Back then, that's what you did to pull a wagon. As you moved forward, your arm moved back, held onto, and pulled it.

Instinct # 6
Shot Sense
(Eliminating unforced errors)

The best way to eliminate unforced errors is to "play the ball...not the shot, or the space!" In other words, don't try to find openings. Just hit your most comfortable shot and openings will find themselves.

Shot sense acts like a governor placed on a car to prevent over accelerating. Also, it's like one placed on your mind to prevent unforced errors. How? By selecting the shot your body is at ease with instead of one the mind thinks it can execute. In other words, an overly ambitious shot that is completely out of whack with your comfort zone.

Remember, the body is bigger than the mind. Pay attention to it! That'll prevent you from making wrong decisions and committing unforced errors. Then, like in the book of Ecclesiastes, you'll discover there's a time for everything. A time when a soft shot makes more sense than a macho smash; a time to take a ball early and skim it over the net ala` Jimmy Connors, and a time to play the ball slightly later, without guiding, to drive it higher and deeper toward the baseline, Ed Moylan like, to send opponents back to the fence and farthest corners of the court.

Proper shot selection is the embodiment of shot sense. Use it and without thought, it'll enable you to "hit your only shot"- the best and most strategic one. But that's not how my friend Stevo did it.

Lessons from Life

Steve is a marvelous athlete and a star hockey player who performed in the cult movie classic "Slap Shot". For him, every shot was a winner. Unfortunately, too many of them didn't live up to his expectations. We always knew, because his disgruntled messages reached us blocks away. Due to his athletic prowess, we scratched heads expecting more from him. However, what we did know was that it only took a rally or two to beat him. Because his overly ambitious shot selection tried to make a goal every time. This technique prevented him from being the hero at his resident seaside club. Being defeated in the club finals yet once again, was too much. During the ceremony, when handed the runner-up trophy, Steve astounded the spectators by flinging the bloody thing into Long Island Sound. That incident, to this day, remains a relished topic of club conversation.

It was five years since seeing Steve. We were to play. He said: "What are you going to teach me, Frankie?" I said, "How about the golden game?" It's a game that will teach you how to eliminate unforced errors like the great Bjorn Borg, and it'll tell you how proficient you are." Steve shocked me by winning 6-3. I never expected him to be so steady. "That's your playing proficiency, Steve. Now let's play a regular set". Back to his usual ways, I beat him rather easily. In no time however, digesting patience and "shot sense"... he learned how to "read the ball", and make the right shot selection, the best one with the least amount of effort.

Like Steve, to eliminate unforced errors, your mind and body need to work together. Steve personified doing that during a perfect set he played without a mistake. Unbelievable! Hitting only the shots his body wanted, I had no chance to track any of them down. It's probably the same technique Henri Cochet, one of the three French Musketeers, used against Bill Tilden. Cochet was the closest approximation of his nemesis. Tilden most admired his shot making stating that even knowing where Henri was aiming, his shots were too good to retrieve.

Some years ago, Chris Evert displayed a slightly different technique playing Pam Shriver in the finals at Amelia Island, Florida. At match point, endless cross-court backhands were exchanged. Chris was ready to hit them forever and determined to do so. But Pam, slightly less practiced at doing that, lost patience and committed the most frequent unforced error that plagued the pros in those days: Hitting down the line when her body wasn't prepared to do so.

Committing the unforced error, Pam lost the match. Why? Because her mind overruled what her body had organized the racket to do... to hit her natural cross court shot yet another time. After the match, sportscaster Cliff Drysdale asked Chris why she hadn't tried to end the point earlier. "Why should I take a chance?" she answered. Think about that comment because you too want to eliminate unforced errors. Why take a chance?

Happily, there are quicker ways to end a point, chiefly by taking the ball on the rise or chipping and coming to net: But not unless your body can do that naturally, and wants to, without reflection from your mind. Right, but when should you hit cross court and when down the line? Most usually, your body will tell you to go cross court and you shouldn't disarrange yourself to do otherwise. So, never let the mind interfere with following the natural path your body has arranged for you to swing into. That'll keep you mentally and physically together. Also, it'll create your best and most effective shot. But let the mind fight the body and you'll end up doing a Stevo. For example:

The majority of players see an opening and "play the shot" instead of "the ball". In other words, a shot that's off balance and overly ambitious, rather than one the body is prepared for: Like when choosing to hit down the line when your body would be more comfortable to hit cross court. Although, two handed players are more apt to produce them... ordinarily only one out of three of those shots will win the point. More often than not, they end up as unforced errors. Why? Because you'll hit against yourself, scrunch, and more likely than not, produce a weaker and less effective shot. One that opponents are anticipating...drooling to hit away from you. So, play the ball and openings will find themselves.

Shot Selection

Fielding a ball on the bounce or in the air... What about it? Most players get this one wrong and mis-hit. Overly anxious, they stretch and try to take a ball in the air that's difficult to reach. A shot which, had they waited, would have been a snap to take on the bounce. So as in life, with a little patience, avoid disturbing the natural synergy your body has established for you to perform. There's only one exception worth violating those rules that I can think of.

It was in the Astrodome when Ken Rosewall and Rod Laver were battling for fifty thousand dollars, a big chunk of money at the time. Shocking the Rocket, "Muscles", as Ken was affectionately called, won the match. But not by employing the elegant free flowing backhand Rod was conditioned to expect. Instead, out of character, Muscles turned into a contortionist, shocked the Rocket out of his socks, and dunked a cramped return away from him. Wouldn't you for fifty grand? Under those conditions, why not! Besides, being up close to the net made it easier for Rosewall to do something unusual. Nastase relished and planned those shots for the fun of confusing the opposition and to make us laugh. But don't make a habit out of trying that funny stuff. Better to hit your only shot.

Above all, no matter how clever your mind thinks it is, don't let it trip you up. In golf or tennis, grooved swings are the answer. But they don't happen by practicing in front of mirrors as some would have you believe. Doing that only encourages you to guide, steer or engineer them. Swings should be totally free, and with the momentum to flow without interruption along their intended path. Watch Federer do it. Even when players are on the side of the court he's hitting into, more often than not, Roger chooses to hit in that direction because, it's the shot his body is prepared for: The most powerful and strategic one.

How to use Shot Sense for doubles

Nobody could get opponents to hit against themselves and commit unforced errors better than the great doubles duo of Bill Talbert and Gardner Mulloy. Two old timers of whom many of you have never known. Rather than smash a serve, Talbert hit smart. Rarely using a second serve, Bill reduced the angle of return by placing it into an opponent's body. Talbert also never tried to end a point outright. Leaving the first and second shot up to you, he strategically placed himself in front of your most comfortable return, causing you to concoct an unwieldy one. By the third shot, if Mulloy hadn't already put you away, Talbert was in position to finish the job.

Together, the two played placement and position to a "T". Constantly keeping their opponents off balance, they forced them to hit awkward, unsure shots. One of their favorite ploys was to tease net players to reach in front of their serving partners for balls they couldn't possibly put away. Now, both on one side of the court, the opponents were left in the unenviable "I" formation. Leaving the other side of their court wide open, they were sitting ducks unable to retrieve just about any shot poked into their court. So take a lesson from two old wily foxes. Especially, don't be overanxious by reaching for a shot that you can't possibly put away. Leave it for your serving partner who will be in better position to handle it.

Using Shot Sense for singles

The one best example of using shot sense that I've ever seen was performed by Arthur Ashe in the 1975 Wimbledon finals. Almost trance-like that day, his shot placement was impeccable. Ninety-three percent of his first serves, rather than overpowering, were strategically placed as were his ground strokes. Playing placement to a "T", all that remained was to position himself in front of his opponent's most comfortable return, and again, with precision, not power, take the ball early and comfortably put it away. Except for occasional lapses, meditating between changeovers brought him back into the zone. Playing like a Buddhist, he took whatever God gave to him for an unparalleled, spectacular and artistic performance. One of which his talented opponent, James Scott Connors was the recipient.

Deprived of favorite shots, uncomfortable ones were all that remained for Jimmy to hit that day. Once you get the hang of "shot sense", the only thing on your mind will be the ball. The way Raphael Nadal, a veritable hitting machine, does and who will do anything to get his mitts on it. His focus on a ball is phenomenal and unlike that of any human I've ever seen. Even Buster, my Labrador retriever, may not have a leg up on him. Nothing distracts either of them. What about you... Where's your mind when you play? Rather than on the ball, most likely it's on how to prepare for, or on where to hit the shot. By now, you shouldn't have to think about that stuff. Your only thought should be to play the ball: The most comfortable and winning one with rhythm, timing and balance.

Instinct # 7
Rhythm Timing And Balance

Smooth, comfortable and on time is the best way to describe this instinct. Instead of using one instinct at a time to play, it ties all of them together. So much so that you could actually play to music and eliminate physical tension and mental anxiety in the process. Imagine, if you can, how it would be to play with ease, complete freedom, like a musician, on time and to the beat.

The way to develop that kind of rhythm - timing and balance, is with easy warm ups, by taking your time, and without trying to knock the cover off the ball.

Warm Ups

Although baseball players warm - up with pepper rallies, unfortunately, most tennis players don't. Many can't sustain a rally. Instead of starting out slowly to sustain one, they prefer to blast away on the first exchange. But that's stupid! I've seen enough tennis elbows or Achilles tendons snap to be respectful of that. Chasing down their wild and unwieldy shots only encourages more of the same. Under those conditions, there's "no chance" in hell to establish rhythm, balance or timing. During warm-ups, what you need to do is to let any ball go that isn't within comfortable reach. Usually, that'll get a ball basher's attention to hit more sensibly.

Tying Instincts Together

Start out with the same easy rhythm and energy to play as when you walk. With so little of it, your rhythm, timing and balance must be perfectly on for a ball to clear the net. But that's a good thing which will draw you to the ball like a magnet and put you into a special groove. Then, without a flicker of thought, having "forgotten the racket", eyes glued to the ball, and with practice, you'll instinctively "read the ball" "measure up to it" "drift and stride" "let the "body organize it" and use "shot sense" to hit with "rhythm, timing and balance."

As with any sport from kick boxing to bowling, those are the instincts that'll enable you to know how to move with total freedom and complete ease. Ala` Ted Williams who used tennis to improve eye-hand coordination to swing a bat. Ala` Annika Sorenstam, Ernie Els, and Fred Couples, who prove that easy, well timed and balanced golf swings travel as far as hard ones.

Often, in tennis, the opposition will provide sufficient power for a simple nudge from you to return a ball with equal force. Unfortunately, young kids who wail the cover off the ball are totally unaware of the game's nuances. Therefore, the energy they expend is wasted. Zing a ball to them and rather than play off your power, they'll neutralize it by trying to hit harder. Sure, the looks and sounds of a ball being whacked may be impressive. But when striking the court, their shots don't carry nearly the pace generated by skilled and truly great strikers of the ball. Skills so finely tuned that you hardly perceive the energy behind their shots. Yet when hitting the ground, the ball explodes! As for rhythm, it's smooth. Thinking destroys it with rules and contorted techniques: Those which will never match up to your proclivity for free and normal movement.

Unfortunately, the beat of most sports is different from the music. What music? Beautiful music I once had students play to. Although wonderful for them, it wasn't so hot for those playing on an adjacent court. Aggravating enough, the beautiful strains of a waltz caused a playing partner and tennis legend friend to bolt off the court and say, "I'm never playing here again!" But he was back the next day. What was his problem? If the fabulous Evonne Goolagong practiced to music, why couldn't he?

Well my pal, like many others, was tuned to a different drummer. The tempo of the music, different than the beat he was used to, destroyed his concentration. Most players, with their grim resolve, couldn't handle it either. Their mindset has little to do with anything rhythmic, or artistic. Grinding - plodding ways leave little room for that. On the other hand, Evonne's play inspired Mary Carillo with another gem to say: "She looks like she's playing barefoot." What a pleasure to see the court used to stage such beautiful, graceful and effective performance. Don't you wish you looked and felt like that when you played?

Concentration versus Awareness

Yogi Berra said, "You can't hit and think at the same time." He was right on! When your mind is on one thing, it'll be off the other. Two things to think about is more than most of us can handle. That's when concentration becomes an instructional hazard. Spending your athletic life stuck on detail prevents you from seeing the forest because of the trees. Your mind has to be totally open, rather than closed, to get the total picture.

Of course, helpful hints are necessary to learn a task. Just as they were when learning to catch, ride a bike or work. However, once you got the hang of those things, performing them became second nature. But when your mind is clogged with detail, awareness goes down the drain. So rather than boost itself, performance whooshes away. Much the same as a musician concentrating on one note at a time will struggle to play a song.

No, to play well, you have to become totally aware. Concentration, rather than an open mind, tends to clog it with detail. To be totally aware, you need to be unconsciously-conscious to use "all" of what you know. That's what will enable you to play by feel - not thought. So be careful not to get stuck on detail. Be more like a typist whose fingers fly over the keys. As for you, allow your mind to sail over the fundamentals... Then play becomes routine.

Also, when instruction doesn't jibe with anything you can relate to, question it until it does. For instance, when you net a ball, don't accept that old adage of "bend your knees" as gospel. But the real reason for netting the ball? Most likely it was that your timing was off, or you reached and met the ball too soon. Meet it on time and it will easily sail over the net. Those errors have nothing to do with not bending knees or watching the ball. To simplify things, here's what you do...

Metronome and tempo like, easy swings are the quickest way to return stinging drives, or to hit them off the tee. Like the swings you use to return practice serves. Usually, they're comfortably and casually returned. My playing partner calls them "garbage shots". But I'll take them any day over missing a ball. Gonzales, in an epic match against the net rushing prowess of Laver, used nothing but garbage shots to return serves. Rod would have preferred drives to easily volley away. But love taps barely clearing the net, made him hit yet another shot. That was smart.

Hitches and Glitches

A swing shorter than your stride is a "hitch". Instead of being full, it's incomplete, held back and cut short. Advocating it to block service returns is stifling and dead wrong! Sure, there are times when no swing is required, but unlike a block, nothing is held back. Total relaxation is all that's required. Then it's merely a matter of placing the racket on the ball. Otherwise, short or long, swings should always be complete, free flowing, and not guided or engineered. But "never" cut them short!

A swing longer than your stride is a "glitch". Overdone, it'll make you rush, throw you off balance, and late. Conversely, swings should be pendulum-like and agree with the body's tempo of drifting and striding. Short ones should be used for bunts, chips, short jabs, half volleys, drop shots, and lightning quick responses. Long ones are for high bouncing balls, swinging volleys, along with serves and slow shots that could put you to sleep.

Mental and Physical Balance

How do you achieve it? By being composed the way Roger Federer is in tennis, or of how Fred Couples and Greg Norman maintain balance in golf. Without an ounce of anxiety and before driving one off the tee, their shoulders, arms, hands and head, are at rest. In tennis, Roger Federer utilizes an abundance of composure to retain balance. The same as you have while standing on a street corner anticipating and expecting a signal to change. Muscles or sinews aren't tingling then. Neither should they when expecting a ball to come your way. Then when you read where it's headed, that's when you react and measure your body up to it.

From tennis to baseball and hockey, ski jumping to you name it... timing is crucial. A New York cabbie waiting to jump a traffic light needs it, too. The anticipation required for a cabbie is equal to that of any sport. For example: The cab slowly drifts forward the way outfielders, tennis players, and swimmers like Michael Phelps do to get the jump on opponents. The instant the signal changes, the driver guns the cab through the light. Rosewall could do the same on a Gonzales serve. That enabled him to beat the big man to net. What an outrageous and magical feat!

However, distractions and dealing with the machinations of opponents can throw you off balance and ruin timing. Distractions like grunts and groans, stalling, wiping glasses, or bouncing a ball ten times before serving. That's annoying stuff! How do you ignore it? The way Rod Laver did.

Opponents, spectators, equipment, playing conditions, nothing bothered him. Like a workman wielding a shovel in the middle of a construction site, he seemed to pay no attention to the neurotic stalling antics of a competitor.

I felt that Rod diverted his attention by watching and thinking about other things such as glancing up at the gallery while an opponent fidgeted before serving. But the micro-second a dastardly opponent made a meaningful move...cat like, the "Rocket" took notice. A wonderful ploy I'd like to ask him about. Like Rod, with zero thought of being annoyed, you should think of something pleasant while an opponent fiddles around.

Then with calm repose, you'll be more aware and ready to react and make "unconscious" returns. What about equipment and playing conditions? Rod had answers for them as well.

As an amateur at Forest Hills, three semi-finalists at the United States Tennis Championships were slip sliding over the wet grass deciding whether or not, spikes should be worn. Not Rod! Without blinking, he simply walked onto the grass without them and did his job.

Another incident occurred during the first "big" money match in the '70's. Madison Square Garden was packed. Ten grand was on the line for Gonzales and Laver. But the Rocket had two opponents that night, the racket he had just endorsed and Pancho Gonzales. Rod's favorite racket was wood. But he was under contract to play with a new aluminum model, an albatross. The first set was awful. Was it the racket, money, or their reputations that were on the line for those two great players? But by the third set, Rod had adjusted to his new equipment. In the fourth, something sounding like a grenade slammed down behind him in the middle of his backswing. Undaunted, I doubt he even noticed. Not only did he finish the shot but went on to win the point - However, not the match. Also, what about the bad back none of us knew about because he never complained? Mind over matter was one more of his winning attributes.

For example: The mind is smaller than your body and directs your moves. Unfortunately, it can easily trip you up. But the body is bigger. Listen to it! When the former agrees, it'll stop resisting the natural order of things. Also, the problems in any sport are easier to spot when both mind and body are on the same page. After all, a rigid mind is no better than an uptight body. You must get rid of both to be free from the whir of constant mental and physical engagement. The kind that causes the bitter parade of sitting-ducks dumped into the net and hit out of bounds. But it's no different in golf. Drives that miss greens and fairways are no laughing matter either.

A cool, calm, and collected mind would prevent many of those errors from occurring. A mind similar to Pancho Segura, a great player from the past, whose admirers chortled while opponents complained about his not having missed an easy put-away in five years. The ploy of Ed Moylan, (another answering machine that never seemed to fail), was never to hit a ball close to a line. To prevent errors, he preferred to hit a yard away. Playing against those two well oiled embodiments of tennis machinery was exasperating. So what about the double faults you feared making, but did? Unlike those guys, your mind tripped you up again!

Seven Habits and Instincts

Years ago, Yannick Noah showed how to avoid mind slip-ups while serving during a Lipton Cup Championship. With phenomenal touch and uncanny placement, his serves carried more surprise than power. Enough to rack up 53 winners and aces against Jimmy Connors. However, that wasn't quite enough for Yannick to win. Jimbo, the great return artist, hung in there. You too can hang in by observing how great talents simply react to play at their highest level. Mentally and physically balanced, rather than contemplate, they just play.

Balance means to be in neutral, mind not cogitating and body not struggling. Whatever the sporting implement, be it bat, racket, ball or club, hold them comfortably. Then use them without doing anything weird or unusual, and until they become part of you. Imagine how free you'll feel not having to tell yourself to get your racket back, assume a restricted stance in the batters box, or struggle when matching yourself up to a tee according to a teacher's dictates. Above all, mentally or physically, don't press. That'll throw you off balance. Composure is the key. Rather than rushing or getting ahead of yourself, learn to take everything in stride. A better way to say it is: Take one thing at a time!

Neither should a muscle or one brain sinew quiver when waiting to receive or to hit a shot. Totally neutralize yourself. Above all, will away affectation and constraint until every mental and physical machination evaporates. Machinations like kicking ego out of the way, or the insecurity from saying things like "I'm sorry," when missing. Sorry? You didn't mean to miss. Except for feeling sorry for yourself, why apologize? I charge a dollar for every sorry I hear. Why? Because it's a negative comment that will drag you down. The sorry I love is the one that hits and dribbles over the net. Sorry... Really?

Finally, especially trust your last second reactions the way Segura did... once in close combat at net as Gonzales set-up for an ominous overhead. No one would have blamed Segura for ducking out of the way, or dropping to a fetal position with the hope of protecting himself from being obliterated. But without blinking, the wily Segura delighted the fans by using Gonzales' power to block a zinging return. It was a return that nearly cut the big man in half as the ball zipped back.

Although few of us have Segura's guts, last second reactions, not mental baggage, can save you. That's because reflexes are far better than the brain for tracking lightning returns, trusting golf swings, or to rapping a pitch. One microsecond of thought about technique, let alone tension, would have been enough to disconnect and prevent Segura's lightning reaction. The lesson...

Disconnects

Disconnects of any sort are detrimental to performance. The transition from serving to fielding a return is one of them. Why? Because when serving, a mind riveted on toss, excessive power, ball placement or technique, will divert your attention from an opponent's return: One that should have been played with tempo and feeling. Instead, your attention was occupied with other things. So, timing went down the drain and caused you to disconnect. Regardless of the sport, disconnects of any kind will be your downfall. Even the slightest mental or physical interruption will make the transition from one move to another more difficult. Thus, tempo and rhythm are destroyed.

Much the same happens when attempting to return delivery of a serve. Equally off putting is a bullet driven at you up at net. Why? Because, embellishment, anxiety, or lack of confidence will do you in! So, how do you hone in on those bomb shells?

The ideal way to "zing 'em back" is with simplicity and ease. That's when your chances to return thunderous serves, meet a flying puck, or contact a 98 mph. pitch will greatly improve. Agassi, a man who says he "concentrates on the beat of his heart" for rhythm, has one of the best service returns. Never rushing, he gets into neutral and pauses before striking the ball.

Pausing is the ability to bring a sporting implement into rest before it's engaged. I call that the pause that refreshes. It's what restores confidence and allows your every play to be taken, not by pressing, but in its own good time. I like the way a friend put it saying:

"Tennis is an easy game, played on a big court with a tiny ball." That wonderful quote came from Edward van Beverhoudt, a USTA national singles champion at age 48. Steady Eddie was right. Simplicity is the essence of greatness. Simple strokes are better than complicated ones... relaxed stances better than rigid ones... as are comfortable and familiar movements better than those which are uncomfortable and unfamiliar

A Game In Confusion

Today, the game of tennis is in disarray. No longer, as in days past, is there one best way to play. Should grips be the traditional "classic" shake-hands technique, or the "contemporary" way? A way of holding a racket more like a frying pan that was once considered laughable and unorthodox. Is that OK? Then why don't lumberjacks turn an ax sideways to fell a tree? No, that would be no different than twisting a foot inward to walk. Similar things happen to golfers whose grips are out of line with the most comfortable swing the body is capable to produce. So which method is right, the classic or contemporary frying pan? Neither as you will see!

The Golden Age

Presently the game resembles the "Golden Age" of the 1920's when there was no right way. Every grip, stance and swing man could concoct was used. That was until Bill Tilden, the great tennis champion, who could guzzle pots of coffee and eat steaks before playing, wrote his classic book How to Play Better Tennis. Considered the one best way to play, his methods became gospel.

Anyone who didn't follow Bill's rules was unorthodox. Today, professionals continue to teach his traditional method. But they also teach the funny grips, swings and open stances we used to call unorthodox. Why? Because of the success well trained athletes have had using styles of their own. However, regardless of style, the racket is still up and out of position. This disconnects your arms from the rest of your anatomy and compels you to pull them back. Completely disorganized, you need to do an Irish River Dance to chase after an exaggerated back-swing. Golfers suffer similar symptoms when they waddle around the tee. It's the jittery stuff that shatters confidence and prevents the physical harmony required for an accurate drive.

Now, without "one" established right way to play, there's lots of confusion about how to teach. Once again, should it be the traditional "shake hands" way, or the helter-skelter "pancake" contemporary style? Either way doesn't matter because the unpardonable sin of picking up the racket has already been taught. Doomed, your arm(s) become broken appendages - a disability opponents relish, because now they know you no longer can handle a ball hit at your feet.

Worse, you have to endure eternal chiding from tennis cronies to "bend your knees" as the solution to get your airborne racket down to meet a low flying ball. That's a technique which gets wearing and increasingly painful with age. It sentences you to attempt things you wouldn't care to coordinate elsewhere.

For example: In any sport, grips can easily become convoluted and uncomfortable. Why? Because your hands, rather than naturally gravitate to a sports implement as they would a hammer or rake, were guided into position. Admit it: That was strange and uncomfortable at first. It still is because grips are always on your mind when they shouldn't be. The more you twist them out of their normal position, the more your mobility becomes compromised and eternally foreign. Therefore, neither the traditional or contemporary methods of teaching have much to do with your normal ways. So, what should you do about that?

Recall the way you sweep a floor or shovel snow. How much thinking does that require? Yet your body and arms work together. That's the perfect example of how you should play. As for machinations, eliminate them in sports, life, behind the wheel, swishing a ball through a hoop, or to line up a puck. Then with little more angst than throwing out the dishwater, let your mantra be to "Let Go and Be Worry Free".

Regardless of the sport, eliminate embellishment, affectation or constraint by: Simply reading the rim of the basket, the speed - spin and direction of a ball - or the bend of a hairpin curve to determine what gear you need to shift down to. Those things tell you when, where, and how to work, and allow your instinctive reactions and best athletic performances to kick in.

So use your God given - natural movements. That's when a sporting implement will enhance performance. But to use one efficiently, you need to know when, where and how to use it to play. That's when the implement in your hand becomes a natural extension of your arm(s) instead of an alien appendage. But, as you're about to see, that's impossible to accomplish with current training techniques in tennis. Be it classic, or contemporary.

Traditional Tennis

Classic or traditional tennis is a knee - busting, by the numbers technique which takes tons of practice and foot shuffling to make somewhat comfortable. Tilden, the father of the concept (like paralysis of analysis in golf) had you doing 12 things just to hit a forehand. That dooms a practitioner to spend a lifetime of thinking and complaining when forgetting to perform one of them. Three grips are taught. Unfortunately, shaking hands is the first one you learn and the beginning of your problems.

Rackets aren't for shaking hands, but to simulate catching and throwing a ball. Shaking hands prevents that...causes your arms to swing open and shut like a rusty gate...forces you to rush the racket back...pins you to the baseline...on bended knee to pick up half volleys and... to madly shuffle your feet to bring a racket into position. Thankfully, you don't shake hands to throw a ball. Neither should you to catch or hit one. The following lesson from life illustrates that point:

In the early eighties at lunch, I asked the organizer of the Legends of Tennis (Rosewall, Newcombe, et-al), what his weakest shot was and about the grip. He said, "For the forehand, I use the Eastern, shake hands grip."
"So, how do you hit it"? I asked. "I watch the ball, take the racket back, turn sideways, bend my knees, shift my weight, and follow through."
"That's a nice traditional forehand" I said. "Now stand up, catch my car keys and toss them back exactly the way you hit your forehand". He replied: "I can't. Trying to throw that way would be ridiculous." So were years of laboring over a traditional forehand. Try standing sideways to catch or throw. Notice how bound up you feel. Normally, without needing reminders, you know better than that.

Contemporary Styles

For years, I taught and played the traditional classic "orthodox" way because, it was passed down (like gospel) from one professional to the next. Until recently, teaching any other way was heretical. Other styles were strange. Entertaining, they made us laugh and were considered funny. But today, well conditioned athletes do use them effectively: All the more power to you if you can. But an easier way is by using gravity to your advantage rather than to fight against it. Not with repetitive drills, but like any worker worth his salt, in the most efficient way

Contemporary styles are easier to learn and require less footwork than the traditional way. However, a very annoying aspect of it also produces more grunts and groans. Unfortunately, this style is body wrenching. Although growing numbers of pros teach this newly accepted and ugly style, it's not for the faint of heart, seniors, or weekend players. It's for well trained athletes. Even so, it's a style which makes them prone to injury.

Holding the racket more like a frying pan and winding your body into a pretzel produces great topspin forehands… But it also pins you further behind the baseline than the traditional style. Today's racket technology encourages that boring style of play. Nonetheless, the downward plane of the racket isn't conducive for returning low backspin drives, or for picking-up half volleys.

Youngsters who start with western forehands usually double up on backhands to avoid changing grips. Then, they have a hard time switching to a bona-fide continental grip which is essential for effective volleys, serves and overheads. Pick a racket up from the ground without adjusting the grip and you'll be close to having a "so-called" extreme western, or frying pan grip: A grip that offers safer margins over the net. But twisting the body - tough on muscles and bones - outweigh any advantage this method has over traditional tennis. I say pros who teach this ugly stuff should be put in jail. Why? Because you don't twist your hands out of position for anything else, so why should you to play? Regardless of the sport, twisted bodies - arms or hands - don't enhance, but cripple performance.

Two of the world's former top women players, Capriati and Hingis exemplified a modification of that style when playing in the 2002 Australian finals. They're extraordinary athletes who can keep a ball in play for ages. That day, both pinned well behind the baseline, their endless rallies looked more like a game of ping - pong. It took forever to win a point. Temperatures of 100+ degrees almost did them in as they hung over railings and sucked in air for wind. Not a pretty sight, but their resolve to endure punishment was admirable. However, had their style of play been as exaggerated as today's grunting - groaning crop of players, I doubt whether they would have been able to endure. So all the more credit to them!

A Game In Confusion

As you can see, this topspin mania is no panacea, and possibly even dangerous! Like when a friend of mine whiffed a forehand and his follow through found its intended target, his nose, scored a TKO and broke it in three places. Life has immutable laws which would have prevented that from happening. Physically fighting against them is a losing battle. So are mean spirited attitudes, fist pumping, hand slapping kid stuff, or macho smashes. None of that will make play better. Neither will it endear players to their audience. Deft angles, drop shots, super lobs, and superb passing shots end the point more artistically and forcefully. Congenial, sportsmanlike attitudes are what the majority of spectators appreciate. However, variety adds color. Although certain ways of playing aren't always good for the athlete, their unique ways of playing are fun to watch.

For instance, as a kid, I remember guys who used the same side of the racket to hit either backhand or forehand. Although a scream, those guys were hard to beat. Much like today's new game, their unique styles had us mumbling under our breath. Why? We were schooled in the game with myriads of things to think about. All they had on their minds was to whack away. That reminds me of a golfer whose only comment about how to play is "see the ball - hit the ball". He's a four handicap.

Unfortunately, ball whacking and well conditioned athletes become insensitive to contortions, grunts, groans and the strain that eternal rallies inflict on them. But when they're sidelined with bad knees, backs, elbows and shoulders, ask about the toll strenuous play has exacted upon them. So think about it...

Twist your foot and you'll walk with a limp. Twist your hands and you'll swing with one. Professionals who've learned to accommodate ungainly grips end up with convoluted swings. Never will they know how easy it is to hit stinging drives with less infringement upon the body. It's criminal to watch the tortured positions they get into to accommodate grips that fight plain and ordinary movement. The kind that agrees with the laws of physics...and with styles that make play easier than those loaded with embellishment, that are tough on knees, mentally and physically exhausting.

A far better style is similar to walking, playing tag, raking the lawn, or chasing the chickens. It's the normal and right thing to do. So why not do yourself a favor: Use your instincts and rid yourself of any awkward and excess baggage. Then your performance will improve, be less taxing, and more enjoyable because your body which is bigger than your brain, will help to coordinate your thinking and movement. Of course, your mind is still in charge, but when it listens and works in harmony with your body, it brings a new dimension to playing any game, along with a winning spirit. All the strange grips and awkward stances you've been taught to use in sports are the exaggerated stuff you never use in life. Make them disappear.

When grips don't match up to your work, not only do they exact a physical toll, but different grips require different swings and places to meet a ball. So if you're not hung-up on grips, why not simplify things by using one that is natural. One which allows the racket to make comfortable catches and throws.

That's the continental grip.

The continental is the only grip which works in harmony with your body. It's the only one that'll allow you to catch and throw with a racket just like you would without one. From ground strokes to serves, it enables you to use a racket as a natural extension of your arm. Also, it eliminates grip confusion and different ways to hit a ball.

In the illustrations that follow, notice that rather than different, all strokes are tied together like a golden thread: One which makes it possible for your step, grip and hit to occur precisely at the same time. That's a place I like to call home. Because like a Musician, doing that will enable you to play the ball with precision. The Natural Approach will show you how.

The Natural Approach

"7" Catches and Throws
(Let's the ball tell you how to hit it)

The racket as a tool, should be used to make catches and throws. The only difference is that with it, you catch and throw at the same time. And the body movements that you're about to see, more than likely, are what you should use to play any sport.

Shots 1&2 - Low forehands and backhands handle balls from the ground up to where your swing (without guiding) throws your racket over the net. That produces natural topspin from ground level up to your waist.

Forehands are easy: Regardless of grip, your step-hit and grip should occur the second the racket sends your body into the ball.

Backhands usually are considered to be more difficult than forehands. Thinking that causes it to be approached more cautiously than a forehand. But it's just a matter of approaching it with the same "tempo" used for forehands. After all, forehands swing one way and backhands swing the other. The only difference with it is the ball should be met further forward for your racket to send the weight of your body onto the ball.

Shots 3&4 – High bouncing forehands and backhands (including swinging -volleys) handle balls above your waist, the net, or your head. Backspin is produced by imitating the way you'd throw a ball down and into the court. Shots taken above the waist give you more court to hit into and less time for your opponent to respond.

High Forehands Shot # 3
With the continental shots (low to high) are met along the same vertical line.

High Backhands Shot # 4
For your step-hit and grip to occur together, backhands must be met along a "graduated line" for the full weight of your body to fall onto the ball.

The Natural Approach 63

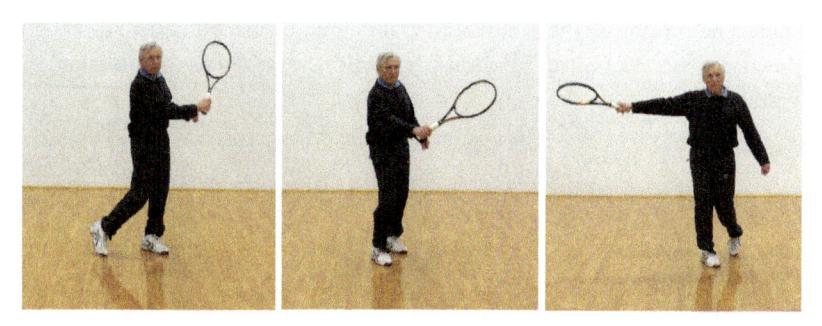

Shot 5&6 - For forehand volleys, swings are automatically shortened by opening, or bending the hand back just as you would to snag a ball, press against a wall, push open a door, or to say hello. Doing those things allows the racket to act like a backboard for a ball to bounce against. But those good things won't happen unless you're in position to do them. Then "if" the racket is not gripped or clutched, a short back-swing will occur as you stride up and over to catch the ball. The grip (just as when a hammer meets a nail) will occur the instant your step and hit come together.

For backhand volleys, the swing is shortened by bending the wrist up and back like a karate chop. Observe how the racket (held in the finger tips) creates a "magic angle" and naturalwaiting stance. An angle you must keep

for protection, comfort, and to make proper contact. Then "if" the racket is not gripped or clutched, a short rocking motion will occur as you drift, or fade out of the way to intercept and drop the weight of your body onto the shot. The motion is the same as a karate chop, or one you'd use to knock down a door. As on "all" backhands, notice how contact occurs along a graduated line.

Shot 7- Overheads and Serves: For overheads, it's just a matter of getting your head directly under the ball to make a comfortable catch. Your body (if relaxed) will turn as the arm winds you up to throw. Then like every other shot, let the racket drop the weight of your body on the ball.

As for serves: The swing is much like golf. For golf, you swing up, and for tennis down. Along with tempo, just as you'd let the club do the work for you in golf, allow that to happen with a racket.

First hold it loosely, the way a pitcher, in finger tips, barely holds onto a ball.

Toss the ball high enough and your tossing arm will arch your back. But for the racket to scratch and collapse behind your back, the tossing arm MUST synchronize with your swing.

If your body is supple, arms and body will work in harmony.
Whip-like, a loose wrist will snap the racket onto the ball to send your entire weight forward. Pros use varying techniques to achieve those results. The easiest and best of them is illustrated as follows :)

As for the toss, everybody makes a big deal about such a tiny toss. Look, if you can sink baskets from 20' away, how tough can such a tiny toss be? So get your mind off the toss. Get it on your target instead. Just as a basketball player eyes the rim of the hoop, and the ball falls through it. That's where the racket

The Natural Approach

snaps and drops your body weight forward-down and onto the ball.

However, don't let a bad toss interfere with the freedom and momentum of your swing. When it goes off track, don't chase after it. Just catch and toss until it finds the path and force of your intended swing. Simply speaking, serving is just a matter of placing the ball in front of your throw.

Above all, never allow the toss to throw your racket off course. That usually happens when the body is tense or jerky. So loosen up your arms and body. Let them flow together to allow your body and toss to do the same direction. Also, remember to discriminately eye your target before serving. That's equally important for the toss to end up in the right place. Above all, don't exaggerate your movements! Make them smooth, free flowing, and no different than when you throw.

Regarding the serve, if practice made it perfect, then my friend, a former number one junior tennis player in the world, would have had the greatest serve. He practiced hundreds of them a day. Unfortunately, all of them wrong. But I won't tell you what he blurted out when any of us mentioned that to him: His reward for not listening was a butter-ball serve that never missed.

During the quarter finals of the United States Championships at Forest Hills, the lad broke the winner's formidable serve five times.
No one else broke it once. Unfortunately, he was unable to hold one of his own. Discouraged, this talented player hung up his racket shortly thereafter.

What is the moral of this story? It's not the years of practice, antiquated teaching techniques passed down from one generation of teaching pros to another, or the teaching camps you attend that make you a better player. It's the quality, not the quantity of practice that counts. When you do things right, a little practice goes a long way.

Therefore, if you're not locked into grips, then I'd urge you to try the natural-neutral continental for every shot from groundstrokes to overheads. The continental has many advantages. For instance:
1. There are no grip changes to distract you.
2. The grip allows you to use gravity to drop a racket down - rather than fighting to lift it up to the ball - with far less energy to throw high bouncing balls down and into the court.
3. It allows you to play the ball earlier, on the rise, rush your opponent, and take advantage of the court by giving you more of it to hit into.
4. It's the natural answer to neutralize topspin drives, and the only grip that's a true extension of your hand. That allows your racket arm to

be at rest, and in a natural — neutral position that works in harmony with your body. Also, it's ideal for picking up half volleys, drop shots close to the net, and to produce easy backhands. Easy backhands...? You bet!

For example: Try swinging a stick back and forth across your body. Which is more difficult... forehand or backhand? Neither of course! Why? Because both swing back and forth as easily as when you walk. The best examples of great backhands were:

Ken Rosewall's one handed continental: A shot that produced brilliant sliced drives on balls above his waist. Rod Laver would occasionally use the continental to hit incredible topspin drives. But to produce them on high backhands fights against gravity, and is tough on the back.

Don Budge used three grips for his great "one handed" backhand. The one he used to return high backhands was unique. He was one of the few players I know to place his thumb behind the handle of the racket to handle them. Those shots, which bother players, were more like batting practice for him. Yet, it was simple, elegant, and produced fabulous line drives. Don would have had a field day playing against today's topspin experts. On the other hand, Roger Federer does just fine with the two other grips that Budge used...The continental for slicing, and the eastern for topspin. But the high bouncing spins that Nadel hits are not as easy for him to handle as a Rosewall slice drive, or a Budge high backhand delivery.

Question: Are two-handed backhands stronger than one? Hardly! The greatest backhands have always been one-handed. Just look at the brilliant backhand the tiny frame of Justine Henin produces. So even if you're a skinny, weak-wristed kid, don't buy into that two handed malarkey.

What about grooving your swing? Naturally grooved swings aren't guided, engineered, or practiced in front of mirrors. Remember? Golfers take note. Thought out swings can never be grooved. Thinking of swings ruins them!

Conversely, when left alone, like the pendulum swing you know, the forward momentum of it forms a natural groove and an automatic follow through. Automatic follow through? Definitely! That has to happen "if" you meet the ball on time. You'll know, because that's when your step, hit and grip are in synch. Try stopping the force generated by that kind of swing and you'll break an arm. Finally, your strokes should be fluid, free, naturally grooved, reactive, and not grimly contemplated. Nothing, including the mind, should get in their way.

Trouble Shooting

"Grip Lock": Unfortunately, too many sports enthusiasts utilize death grips when playing a sport. In "grip lock", they're always playing with the brakes on. It happens when the whites of your knuckles appear. Say like when trying to extract blood from a steering wheel while driving. Yet, you wouldn't dream of gripping a hammer before it meets the nail. That's "grip lock"! Aside from creating "physical tension" it causes arms to be ripped away from the body, is tiring, and stifles your reactions. How do I know?

When I was a kid, all I heard was watch the ball, get your racket back, bend your knees, squeeze the racket, and follow through. You need to be a magician to coordinate all those things. Plus the tension caused by them will hinder any kind of swing, pitch, punch, dive, jump shot, or drive.

Excessive thought is another bugaboo to hinder reaction. It's an instructional hazard that causes affectation and constraint - two enemies you don't need! So what's the solution?

Here are a few reminders: Hold, don't Grip! Make a sporting implement an extension of your hand, one which is no different from any tool you'd hold. Above all, don't prematurely grip or squeeze. Just as when you strike any object, grips (without help) automatically occur on contact. Conversely, thinking about when and how to grip is a distraction, to say nothing about the tension it causes.

Just as a sledgehammer is held without tension, sporting tools should be held lightly as a pencil, a surgeon's scalpel, or the brush of an artist. The cardinal rule is to hold an implement properly for the work it's suited to do. Like how a racket "should" be held to pick up, catch and throw a ball. When done right, the technique is rather simple. With far less bending, it's no different than picking-up a piece of paper. Compare that to the knee busting stuff some teaching pros advocate.

As for grips, John McEnroe's spaghetti grip, barely held onto, is a marvelous example of how quickly, lightning like, it finds the ball. Use any tool properly, sporting or otherwise, and it will become part of you. In tennis, baseball or golf, grip happens last and precisely when a swing throws you off of one foot, onto the other, and into a ball. Otherwise, you're out of synch.

"The wobbles": A miss-timed ball with a loosely held racket may wobble a little. Even with the wobbles, a lightly held racket is better than a strangled one. Why? Because it deflects the force of a mis-hit or badly timed ball from your arm. Also, it allows your body to be in neutral and free from doing anything unusual. You know, "casual like" until the split second you need to react.

"Overdoing": Trying to knock the cover off the ball (encouraged today) is a mistake: One similar to overloading a shovel with dirt to make it unwieldy to use. That's over-trying! Instead, do what the old time Aussies did. Go out to "nudge a few" like a dog may do to you. Doing that, those guys, along with Margaret Court, barely used any energy to pulverize the ball. With lightning "rote" reactions, they used any opponent's strength against them. The harder you hit, the less they had to do.

Power comes not from slugging, but from rhythm, balance and timing. The same pro women golfers use to knock out 260 yard drives. That's why Julius Boros, one of the most natural golfers ever, titled his book Swing Easy-Hit Hard. Roger Federer, equally natural at tennis, plays with no more thinking, trying, or tension than you'd use to swat a fly. Roger moves no differently on the court than off. Playing by feel, he allows his body to direct his moves.

So, return to your normal ways to establish a marker for you to identify awkward, wasted energy or motion. Do that and you'll no longer need someone to remedy problems because they'll reveal themselves. Then, as the song "Accentuate the Positive, Eliminate the Negative" urges, the stuff that has prevented you from moving around the way you'd like, will disappear. It will also give insight into why doing less will enable you to do more.

Above all, get rid of expert advice that strays away from your comfort zone or doesn't jibe with any movement you know. Especially remember your free flowing ways that require no more thought than when you wash your face. No one needs to tell you how to do that because, nobody knows how to do it better.

Use those techniques and play will become second nature. That's when you'll move with the precision of a fine Swiss watch, and the way God intended for you to move. During the process, you'll have discovered the best therapy for aches and pains.

Parting Shots

No one had more fun when playing on the court than Nastase. He was brilliant, as when playing Harold Soloman at a River Oaks tournament in Texas some years ago. Solomon, a very solid player, could hit moon balls all day and virtually put you to sleep. Knowing that and anticipating a marathon match, players jested with Ilie to bring his lunch. Playing fabulously he made short order of the first set and held a comfortable lead in the second. Then things begin to change. Unhappy with the quality of the balls, Nasty presented them to the chair umpire to be replaced. When his request was denied, he kicked a ball into the stands. From that point on, the match was no longer fun for Nasty, it was over.

Afterwards, the cameras followed Nasty as he entered the parking lot behind the chair umpire and swore at him in several languages. It was the funniest thing producer Harry Moses ever filmed for 60' Minutes. Interviewing Ilie, Mike Wallace asked why he did those things. "I can't help myself"', Nasty appropriately responded. But hopefully you can.

Enjoying the Game

A happy attitude removes tension. How do I know? Once, during a tournament match, tennis acquaintances I hadn't seen for years passed my court and lifted my spirits. Greeting them with waves and "hellos" between points gave me a boost big enough to begin playing out of my mind. Being so jubilant was devastating to my opponent. That reminds me of Tilden's comments. "Never make a serious business out of winning". He said, "The fascination of playing the game is paramount. Also, play without the fear of losing and because it's fun. Otherwise, don't play at all!" Strong words from the master that carry a lot of truth, even if big business tennis has put them out of style.

Sadly, the game's gentle side has vanished, like the smiles of a Manuel Santana in defeat and of his tears in victory. Now winning is everything, even for some recreational players. Except for vanity and ego, why are they so heavy spirited on the court? That type of mentality destroys play rather than improves it. We already have too many professionals with grim resolve who can't smile or take a joke.

Playing in the Zone
(Getting mind and body out of the way)

When friends laugh and say "You're unconscious", and you're playing buddy mutters, "That's not you hitting the ball", you must be playing spontaneously and out of your mind. Try as you might to duplicate such performance, you can't. Those brilliant moments are like trying to hold onto vapor, which reminds me of an experience I had forty years ago.

On a foggy New England morning after a very long day as tennis pro, manager, bookkeeper, public relations man, and janitor, I was trying to get a new indoor tennis facility off the ground. After twelve hours of lessons and playing with prospective members, who should walk in after midnight but my tennis "junkie" pal Irving. "Let's play," he said. Why not?

Turning the inside fans on draws in the outside fog. The place looked more like a graveyard than a tennis court. I almost fell on my face after hitting the first return. My physical and mental exhaustion made trying and thinking impossible. No longer would such things bother me because, almost playing by rote, my instincts took over. Suddenly play becomes as simple as snagging a ball. In total disbelief, I get the most out of my shots with the least amount of effort. Did I feel like Ashe on that special day against Jimbo at Wimbledon? You bet! But it's not necessary to be exhausted to play that way.

However, that night taught me the lessons necessary to put me in the zone: Lessons minus the mental baggage that louses up and prevents instincts from kicking in. Instincts, as Tom, my doubles partner, would say, "That you do with a feeling of no feeling".

Parting Shots

With an empty peaceful mind - total physical composure - pro golfer like... the only feeling to have is of the beautiful shot you envision and the rhythm, timing and balance you'll use to make it.

Barely trying, like magic, that's when the ball goes sailing miles down the fairway, to the farthest ends of the court, or over the wall when swinging a bat. Then you're playing in the zone, getting the most out of your shots, and "playing the way nature intended". However, it is imperative to play by feel, and to instinctively react without an ounce of mental or physical interference. In plain English, you simply need to "forget yourself". Then unconsciously use the simple-easy motions in this book with Rhythm, Timing and Balance. God Bless!

ADDENDUM

New Technology:

New technology has allowed players to play differently. Light rackets (more like ping-pong paddles) are easier to swing. High tech strings add power – spin and make weaknesses disappear. "I couldn't miss a ball for two hours", said Agassi the first time he used one of the new rackets. "It makes players great."

Many of today's authorities would argue that the strings and racket technology make the game easier, and it becomes harder to miss, but strongly believe that the strokes are excellent as well. All of this sounds wonderful, but what's really going on?

Although the technology allows pros to rifle shots from well behind the baseline, skills haven't necessarily improved. However, they do make endless strategic-less rallies and record breaking matches boring: when you've seen one, you've seen them all. But like the Golden, Traditional, or Contemporary games of the past, the pain and endurance required of players will cause the current rage to change as did those of former years.

Djokovic seemed to allude to the insanity of it all. Exhausted, hobbling and barely able to stand after a marathon 2012 Australian semi-final against Murray, he graciously motioned to Laver and said, "Perhaps players should learn to play more like you." That thought may have been reinforced next by a grueling record-breaking six hour final duel against Nadal. Spectacular as it was, it confirmed that things must change. Otherwise, players will continue to self destruct, and astute spectators will turn to sports of more interest. But hope remains by **Playing in the zone** and, **Moving the way nature intended.**

For more information about illustrations and
"The Unconscious Athlete"
log on to:
www.unconsciousathlete.com

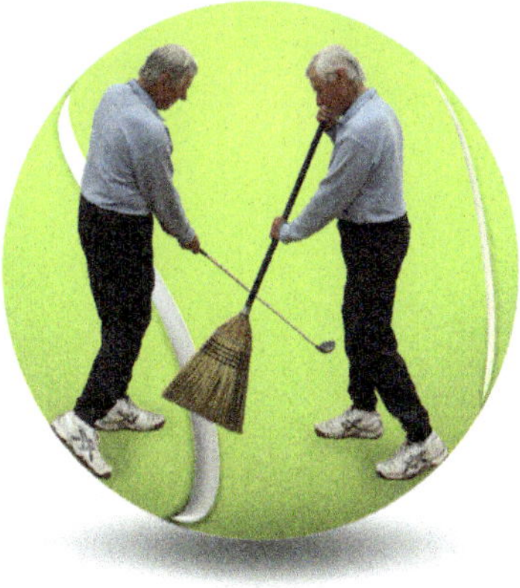